RAND

Science and Technology Policy Institute
Drug Policy Research Center

IMPROVING ANTI-DRUG BUDGETING

PATRICK MURPHY

LYNN E. DAVIS

TIMOTHY LISTON

DAVID THALER

KATHI WEBB

Prepared for the
Office of National Drug Control Policy

The research described in this report was conducted by RAND's Science and Technology Policy Institute and Drug Policy Research Center staff for the Office of National Drug Control Policy under Contract ENG-9812731.

Library of Congress Cataloging-in-Publication Data

Improving anti-drug budgeting / Patrick Murphy ... [et al.].
    p. cm.
    "MR-1262-ONDCP."
    Includes bibliographical references.
    ISBN 0-8330-2915-0
    1. Narcotics, Control of—United States—Finance. 2. Drug abuse—United States—Prevention—Finance. 3. United States. Office of National Drug Control Policy—Appropriations and expenditures. I. Murphy, Patrick.

    HV5825 .I5353 2000
    353.3'7—dc21

                                                                00-045832

RAND is a nonprofit institution that helps improve policy and decisionmaking through research and analysis. RAND® is a registered trademark. RAND's publications do not necessarily reflect the opinions or policies of its research sponsors.

Published 2000 by RAND
1700 Main Street, P.O. Box 2138, Santa Monica, CA 90407-2138
1200 South Hayes Street, Arlington, VA 22202-5050
RAND URL: http://www.rand.org/
To order RAND documents or to obtain additional information,
contact Distribution Services: Telephone: (310) 451-7002;
Fax: (310) 451-6915; Internet: order@rand.org

In 1988, Congress created the Office of National Drug Control Policy (ONDCP) to coordinate the nation's antidrug programs and activities. Each year the president submits a drug control budget requesting funds to carry out his overall National Drug Control Strategy. That budget is based on certifications the ONDCP Director has made as to the adequacy of the budget requests of the over 50 departments engaged in antidrug activities. What confidence can Congress have in these budget figures? This study undertook to answer this question through an analysis of the drug-budget methodologies used in ten antidrug agencies. Our conclusion is that real problems exist in seven of these cases, and steps need to be taken in the future for the ONDCP Director to be able to carry out his statutory responsibilities.

ONDCP sponsored this study. It was conducted at RAND through the Drug Policy Research Center and the S&T Policy Institute.

THE DRUG POLICY RESEARCH CENTER

The Drug Policy Research Center was established in 1989 to conduct the empirical research, policy analysis, and outreach needed to help community leaders and public officials develop more effective strategies for dealing with drug problems. The center builds on a long tradition of RAND research characterized by an interdisciplinary, empirical approach to public policy issues and rigorous standards of quality, objectivity, and independence. The Ford Foundation and other foundations, as well as government agencies, corporations, and individuals, support the Center. Dr. Audrey Burnam and Dr. Martin Iguchi codirect the Drug Policy Research Center. The

Drug Policy Research Center is a joint endeavor of RAND Criminal Justice and RAND Health.

THE SCIENCE AND TECHNOLOGY POLICY INSTITUTE

Originally created by Congress in 1991 as the Critical Technologies Institute and renamed in 1998, the Science and Technology Policy Institute is a federally funded research and development center sponsored by the National Science Foundation and managed by RAND. The Institute's mission is to help improve public policy by conducting objective, independent research and analysis on policy issues that involve science and technology. To this end, the Institute supports the Office of Science and Technology Policy and other Executive Branch agencies and offices, and consults broadly with representatives from private industry, institutions of higher education, and other nonprofit institutions. Bruce Don is the Director of the S&T Policy Institute.

CONTENTS

TABLES

The United States spends over $16 billion a year to fight drugs, or so the president reports in his drug control budget. What confidence can Congress have that this budget accurately reflects federal expenditures on antidrug activities?

In an effort to answer this question, the ONDCP Director, who has responsibility for preparing the national drug control budget, asked RAND to evaluate the methodologies ten federal agencies use to compile their antidrug budgets.[1] These agencies were selected because of their significant role in the drug war and because of ONDCP's questions about the validity of their methodologies. For the year chosen for this research, Fiscal Year (FY) 1998, these agencies represented more than half of the federal drug control budget.

BUDGETING OVERVIEW

Congress created ONDCP in 1988 and gave it broad responsibility to direct and coordinate the nation's drug policy. The director annually presents his Drug Control Strategy to Congress, along with a federal drug control budget, which he must certify as adequate to carry out that strategy. The nature of the antidrug effort, combined with the

---

[1]The agencies examined were the Bureau of Prisons, U.S. Coast Guard, U.S. Customs Service (Customs), U.S. Department of Defense, U.S. Department of Education, Federal Bureau of Investigation (FBI), Immigration and Naturalization Service (INS), Health Care Financing Administration, Substance Abuse and Mental Health Services Administration (SAMHSA), and Department of Veterans Affairs (DVA).

structure of the federal budget system, significantly complicates the effort to assemble the drug control budget.

The challenge is essentially to separate out a subset of resources from an organization's total budget, drawing lines that demarcate what should be considered "drug control" and what constitutes "everything else." The product of those efforts is the collection of estimates that the president presents to Congress. These estimates are calculated using a variety of methods, involving the exercise of considerable discretion. How that discretion is exercised can also reflect fundamental policy decisions. Refining drug-budget methodologies is therefore more than an accounting exercise.

Raising the issue of the reliability of the drug-budget figures in turn raises the question of how much precision and confidence are needed. The answer depends on the purposes the budget is to serve: financial control, planning, management, or political advocacy. Initially, the drug control budget was essentially a political document with little need for precision. The responsibilities outlined in ONDCP's authorizing statute, as well as the institution of a performance measure system, both suggest an explicit planning and management role and the need for greater accuracy. But do the estimates that comprise the drug control budget reflect federal antidrug expenditures, and are they reliable enough to support ONDCP's responsibilities? Over the 11-year existence of the ONDCP, it is a question that has garnered little attention. But if the methodologies are flawed, ONDCP's efforts would seem futile, and the American people are being misled.

ONDCP has made the most significant, concerted effort in the federal government since the program budgeting era of the 1960s to collect budget data across organizational lines and has used the information to manage a program. The uniqueness of ONDCP's effort, however, does not render it irrelevant. Interest has arisen recently in defining agency expenditures in such politically charged areas as counterterrorism and nonproliferation. Understanding how agencies have approached the task in deriving estimates of their antidrug expenditures should prove instructive for those given responsibilities for defining crosscutting budgets in the future.

REVIEW OF METHODOLOGIES

RAND analyzed the antidrug budget methodologies of the ten agencies using the following criteria:

- Did the methodology use a systematic approach that was based on a clear definition of what programs were included, and was it then documented, replicable, and reconcilable with the figures reported for other missions?

- Did the methodology use empirical data, and was the program information current?

- Were the methodologies consistent, accurate, and understandable?

In three cases, the methodologies were appropriate and provided a reasonable estimate of the resources being devoted to antidrug efforts. The Coast Guard has developed a dynamic model for calculating antidrug expenditures based on a timekeeping system and on tracing the costs of these operations. The Bureau of Prisons compiles data each year on the percentage of its inmate population sentenced for drug offenses. That percentage is then multiplied by the total costs to determine the antidrug expenditures. The Department of Defense, through its planning, programming, and budgeting system, determines which military assets will be dedicated to antidrug activities, and their costs are then included in its counterdrug budget.

Three of the agencies began with a logical framework for estimating drug expenditures, but the implementation was flawed. In one of its divisions, the FBI uses a timekeeping system to determine the percentage of time expended on drug activities and then calculates its antidrug budget based on this percentage. Problems arise in the other divisions, where the FBI has defined a complicated methodology based on judgments about the types of investigations that are "potentially" antidrug. The Department of Veterans Affairs identifies patients suffering from drug addiction and assigns the costs of their substance abuse treatment to the antidrug budget. A significant problem emerges, however, when the department goes on to allocate to its antidrug budget the costs of other kinds of medical care for the same patients. The Department of Education uses client profiles and cost data to estimate the portion of its total budget that comprises antidrug services and grants. Problems arise in their inclusion of programs that may be drug related but do not provide drug treatment or prevention services.

The antidrug methodologies in the other agencies had serious deficiencies. In the cases of INS and Customs, the methodologies are based largely on educated guesses. The Substance Abuse and Mental Health Services Administration (SAMHSA) methodology is a collection of arbitrary assumptions and rules. The methodology the Health Care Financing Administration uses is based on patient diagnoses and costs, but the patient data are taken from a 1983 survey.

ANTIDRUG BUDGET IS INFLATED

What these methodological problems mean for the overall size of the national drug control budget is uncertain. For the agencies that fail to use empirical data, it is obviously not possible to say whether the budget figures are high or low.

The antidrug budgets for the Coast Guard and the Bureau of Prisons reflect quite accurately the resources being expended. The Department of Defense method of omitting certain personnel costs has the effect of underestimating the overall amount of funds for counterdrug activities.

In three agencies, Education, Veterans, and SAMHSA, the methodologies produce inflated antidrug budgets, the cumulative effect of which is to inflate the overall FY 1998 antidrug budget of $16 billion by over $1 billion. The largest discrepancy emerges in the Department of Veterans Affairs. Including the other medical care costs for drug abuse patients inflates its budget by $710 million, or 66 percent. As these three agencies focus on reducing the demand for drugs, the effect is that the ONDCP Director's antidrug budget in FY 1998 for these prevention and treatment programs was about 20 percent less than reported to the American public.

The ONDCP Director cannot effectively plan programs to reduce the demand for illicit drugs or hold agencies accountable for their performance with a margin of error of 20 percent in his estimate of available resources.

RECOMMENDATIONS

The ONDCP Director will only be able to carry out his legislatively mandated responsibilities and use the antidrug budget to plan and hold agencies accountable by defining new methodologies to produce reliable budget figures. The recommendations that follow specifically address the ten agencies reviewed, but the general principles should be applicable to all the agencies reporting antidrug expenditures.

- **Methodologies should be based on a systematic approach.** While calculating a drug budget will necessarily be a function of estimates and assumptions, the process needs to be based on a systematic approach that is well documented, replicable, and reconcilable with other figures reported for the agency's missions. The most important step in developing such an approach would be for ONDCP to define explicitly what constitutes an antidrug activity and then ensure that this definition is applied consistently within and to the extent possible across all the antidrug agencies.

- **Methodologies should be empirically based and current.** The drug budget methodologies should be based on empirical data, something more than guesses or expert judgments. Equally important, the representation of the resources devoted to the antidrug effort should be accurate.

  Toward this end, the Coast Guard's system of tracking how much time is spent on different missions provides a possible model for agencies involved in drug interdiction and law enforcement. The FBI's system, which allows agents to record the time spent on different assignments, now needs to be expanded so that agents in all units will be able to report the time they spend on antidrug investigations. Such a permanent and elaborate timekeeping system may be too costly for either the INS or the Customs Service. Such a significant change, though, may not be necessary. Each could assess personnel time utilization by periodically sampling a group of inspectors and investigators and/or the assets they use.[2] By conducting such a timekeeping audit at

---

[2]These agencies may already conduct similar audits, but no systematic efforts appear to be under way to gauge time utilization for these purposes.

regular intervals, the two agencies could identify how their resources are allocated to different program activities. This distribution could then be used to calculate the share of the budget devoted to antidrug efforts.

Grant-providing agencies could follow a similar strategy in attempting to gather empirical data on how recipients use the funds distributed to them. Requiring all recipients to report, for the purpose of developing a drug budget number, on every dollar they receive would be overly burdensome for both the agencies and the recipients. Many of these grant programs, however, do have ongoing evaluations of a subset of their recipients. Including in these evaluations a component that attempts to assess how resources are being utilized relative to the categories in the federal drug budget does not appear to be onerous. In short, using empirical information collected from a sample of program participants would be more desirable than relying on a collection of percentages chosen in a relatively arbitrary fashion.

- **Similar methodologies should be derived from common principles.** Each of the drug budget methodologies was unique to the agency. No consistency existed overall or even in the cases of similar activities, such as law enforcement or treatment. ONDCP should work with the agencies to introduce common principles for developing drug budget methodologies, categorizing these as follows:

  — The **interdiction and law enforcement agencies** should determine how their resources are deployed relative to their various missions, and then apply the shares to the associated costs of the relevant assets and personnel.

  — The **direct service providers** should identify the individuals involved with illegal drugs and then account for the share of costs associated with providing the services, e.g., treatment, to those individuals.

  — The **grant agencies** face more difficult challenges in estimating how the recipients are spending their funds. But they should develop common guidelines, e.g., they could choose to count services provided to all individuals suffering from addiction to both alcohol and illicit drugs.

- **Public presentation of methodologies should be consistent, accurate, and understandable.** Each year, ONDCP publishes a budget summary to accompany the National Drug Strategy, which includes a summary of how the agency calculates its drug budget. The public presentation of the drug budgets of all ten agencies raised problems; in some cases, the information was incomplete, and in others, the methodology was not accurately presented. ONDCP should work with the agencies to ensure that these descriptions are both accurate and understandable, and at a minimum, the methodology reports should in fact be the one the agency uses.

BENEFITS OF IMPROVED METHODOLOGIES

Notwithstanding the costs to implement these recommendations, significant benefits would result. By establishing some common principles to guide the agencies in developing their methodologies, the ONDCP Director will be better positioned to compare the budgets of agencies performing similar tasks and to make trade-offs, within budget limits. More consistency gives agencies an opportunity to learn from each other in their efforts to achieve more precision. The most important benefit is that it will enable the ONDCP to use the drug budget more effectively to implement strategies and hold agencies accountable for their performance.

Given the nature of federal drug budget activities and the structure of the federal budget system, the drug control budget will necessarily be a collection of estimates, calculated using different methods and involving the exercise of some discretion. But the reliability of its figures can be significantly improved. The basis upon which these figures are derived can be made more transparent and understandable to Congress. This is essential for the ONDCP Director to be able to carry out his statutory responsibilities to direct and coordinate the nation's antidrug programs and for the American people to have confidence as to what resources are being spent on antidrug activities.

ACKNOWLEDGMENTS

The authors would like to thank many people for their assistance on this project. Peter Reuter was very helpful in getting the project under way and then in giving us a challenging and insightful review. Our other reviewer, Robert Levine, held us to a high standard of analysis and helped us with our overall presentation. Lisa Sheldone, the Science and Technology Institute administrator, was invaluable in helping us through the various stages of contracting and publication. With a remarkable calmness and expertise, Viki Halabuk put the entire manuscript together.

We would also like to thank the staff of ONDCP, who worked closely with us in our efforts to understand the various department and agency methodologies. John Carnevale, former Director of the Programs, Budget, Research and Evaluation, was especially helpful in giving us guidance and support. Finally, we would also like to acknowledge the information and assistance that the budget officials in the ten agencies provided us.

ABBREVIATIONS

AC&I	Acquisition, Construction, and Improvements
APA	American Psychiatric Association
BOP	Bureau of Prisons
CHIP	Children's Health Insurance Program
CTA	Central Transfer Account
DOD	Department of Defense
DOJ	Department of Justice
DVA	Department of Veterans Affairs
ED	U.S. Department of Education
FBI	Federal Bureau of Investigation
FTE	Full-time-equivalent
FY	Fiscal year
HCFA	Health Care Financing Administration
INS	Immigration and Naturalization Service
ISIS	Integrated Surveillance Intelligence System
KDA	Knowledge and development programs
MILPER	Military personnel
NIDRR	National Institute on Disability and Rehabilitation Research

O&M	Operations and maintenance
OAS	Office of Applied Studies
OCE	Organized criminal enterprise
OE	Operating expenses
OMB	Office of Management and Budget
ONDCP	Office of National Drug Control Policy
OPTEMPO	Operational tempo
OSD	Office of the Secretary of Defense
PA&E	Program Analysis and Evaluation
PERC	Program Evaluation and Resources Center
RDT&E	Research, Development, Test, and Evaluation
S&E	Salaries and expenses
SAMHSA	Substance Abuse and Mental Health Services Administration
SAPPBG	Substance Abuse Performance Partnership Block Grants
SDFSC	Safe and Drug-Free Schools and Communities
TURK	Time Utilization Record-Keeping System
VCCLEA	Violent Crime Control and Law Enforcement Act
VCRTF	Violent Crime Reduction Trust Fund
VR	Vocational Rehabilitation

Chapter One

INTRODUCTION

The United States spends over $16 billion a year on the war on drugs, or so the president reports in his drug control budget. What confidence can Congress and the American people have that this budget accurately reflects federal expenditures on antidrug activities?

In an effort to answer this question, the Director of the Office of National Drug Control Policy (ONDCP), who has responsibility for preparing the drug control budget, asked RAND to evaluate the methodologies that ten agencies use in compiling their antidrug budgets. This monograph presents the findings from that review.

The agencies examined were the Federal Bureau of Prisons (BOP), the U.S. Coast Guard, the U.S. Customs Service (Customs), the Department of Defense (DOD), the Department of Education (ED), the Federal Bureau of Investigation (FBI), the Immigration and Naturalization Service (INS), the Health Care Financing Administration (HCFA), the Substance Abuse and Mental Health Services Administration (SAMHSA), and the Department of Veterans Affairs (DVA). They were selected because they play a significant role in the drug war and because ONDCP had asked about the validity of their methodologies. For the year chosen for this research, fiscal year (FY) 1998, these agencies represented more than half of the federal drug control budget. (See Table 1.1.)

From the perspective of evaluating drug budget methodologies, the coverage of these ten agencies is even more extensive. Four of the antidrug agencies and programs are acknowledged to be 100-percent drug control. These four—the Drug Enforcement Administration,

Table 1.1

Agency Antidrug Activities FY 1998

Agency	Drug-Control Expenditures ($M)	Share of Total Drug Budget (%)	Primary Drug-Control Activities
BOP	1,935.2	12.1	Incarceration of drug offenders
Coast Guard	401.6	2.5	Law enforcement, interdiction
Customs	606.4	3.8	Law enforcement, interdiction
DoD	847.7	5.3	Interdiction, international programs
ED	685.3	4.3	Prevention
FBI	825.4	5.2	Law enforcement, investigations
HCFA	360.0	2.2	Treatment
INS	400.3	2.5	Law enforcement, interdiction
SAMHSA	1,319.6	8.3	Treatment
VA	1,097.2	6.9	Treatment
Total	8,478.7	53.1	

SOURCE: ONDCP (1998b).

the ONDCP, the Interagency Crime and Drug Enforcement, and the Department of State's Bureau of International Narcotics Affairs—total over $2.2 billion. The ten selected agencies and those considered to be 100 percent drug-control accounts, taken together, represent over two-thirds ($10.7 billion) of the FY 1998 drug budget. Nevertheless, more than 50 agencies are involved in antidrug activities, and 12 of these reported drug-control expenditures of over $100 million in FY 1998.[1]

FY 1998 was chosen as the base year for evaluating these antidrug budget methodologies, so that RAND researchers could trace the

---

[1]The agencies include the Centers for Disease Control and Prevention; the National Institutes of Health; the Federal Judiciary; the Office of Justice Programs; the Department of Justice (DOJ) Asset Forfeiture Fund; the U.S. Attorneys; the Community Politics program; Federal Prisoner Detention; the U.S. Marshals Service; the Department of Housing and Urban Development; the Bureau of Alcohol, Tobacco, and Firearms; and the Treasury Forfeiture Fund. For more-detailed information on these agencies, see ONDCP (1999a).

evolution of the drug budget numbers from the initial agency submission to the ONDCP in the summer of 1996, through the executive and congressional budget processes, to the end of the fiscal year.

The assessment of methodologies began with a paper audit of the publicly available documents (the ONDCP budget summary and agency congressional budget submissions) and other unpublished materials from ONDCP budget files. The goal was simply to reconcile the numbers with the reported methodology. The next step was to evaluate the antidrug methodologies in terms of the following criteria:

- Did the methodology use a systematic approach that was based on a clear definition of what programs were included, and was it then documented, replicable, and reconcilable with the figures reported for other agency missions?

- Did the methodology use empirical data, and was the program information current?

- Were the methodologies consistent, accurate, and understandable?

Researchers attempted to balance their assessments of the appropriateness of the methodologies with reasonable expectations regarding accounting practices and data collection. For example, an agency's existing system of accounts and subaccount levels of budget categories was considered to be an immutable constraint. Budget accounts, as recognized by the U.S. Treasury and the Office of Management and Budget (OMB), are established by statute. Budget *decision units*, which typically correspond to subaccount-level programs or activities, are created by the agency in accordance with its organizational structure. Agencies were not expected to change the structures of their budget systems in an effort to provide a better accounting of drug dollars, even though some agencies have established or identified decision units dedicated primarily or solely to antidrug activities. In addition, researchers did not envision radical changes in the collection of new program data solely for the purpose of calculating antidrug resources.

On the basis of the paper audits, researchers prepared initial reviews of the selected agencies and shared them with ONDCP analysts.

RAND researchers then met with budget officials in each of the agencies to discuss these assessments and to clarify any issues surrounding the agency's formulation of the drug budget. After the discussions and, in some cases, follow-up contacts, final budget methodology reviews were prepared.

ORGANIZATION

The next chapter of this monograph provides a historical overview of the role and experiences of the ONDCP in compiling antidrug budgets and discusses that experience in terms of the role of budgets and budgeting in general. Chapters Three through Twelve each describe one of the ten agencies. Each chapter begins with a description of the agency's mission, the role its antidrug efforts play within that mission, and how the mission relates to ONDCP's goals (see below). Each then goes on to describe the drug budget and the methods the agency uses to calculate the figures, then ends with our analysis and conclusions. The final chapter summarizes the investigation's conclusions and offers recommendations for developing future drug budget methodologies.

ONDCP GOALS

The specific goals referred to in each chapter are laid out in ONDCP (1998c):

Goal 1:   Educate and enable America's youth to reject illegal drugs as well as alcohol and tobacco.

Goal 2:   Increase the safety of America's cities by substantially reducing drug-related crime and violence.

Goal 3:   Reduce the health and social costs to the public of illegal drug use.

Goal 4:   Shield America's air, land, and sea frontiers from the drug threat.

Goal 5:   Break foreign and domestic drug sources of supply.

Chapter Two

BUDGETING OVERVIEW

ONDCP'S STATUTORY RESPONSIBILITIES

Congress created ONDCP as part of the Executive Office of the President in 1988 (PL 100-690). That legislation, and subsequent amendments, gave the office broad responsibility to direct and coordinate the nation's drug policy (PL 105-20). But the statutes provided relatively limited authority to carry out this responsibility.

This chapter describes the statutory authorities of the office and the process ONDCP uses to carry out its responsibilities, then discusses why it is difficult to account for antidrug resources that cut across organization and programmatic lines. The chapter concludes by placing ONDCP's experiences in a broader theoretical and historical context.

The ONDCP Director is charged with the establishment and coordination of drug policy for all federal agencies with programs that contribute to antidrug efforts (see 21 USC 1703 (a)).[1] ONDCP's authorizing statute requires the director to set priorities and objectives annually for accomplishing the president's antidrug goals. The central vehicle for carrying out this responsibility is the National Drug Control Strategy. Each year, ONDCP must prepare this strategy for submission by the president to Congress. According to the authorizing statute, the strategy must cover the following (see 21 USC 1705):

---

[1] This authority extends to federal efforts that address illegal drugs and programs seeking to prevent or treat alcohol consumption by individuals under the age of 21.

- comprehensive long-term goals and short-term objectives along with outcome measurements
- estimates of the number of drug users and of the amount of drugs being produced and distributed
- a review of state and local activities
- an assessment of the consequences of drug use indicators of treatment availability and effectiveness by state
- an assessment of federal technology programs
- a list of all people consulted in the preparation of the strategy.

To accompany the strategy, ONDCP is also required to submit a federal drug control budget. This budget requests the resources necessary to implement the strategy and accomplish its stated objectives. Toward this end, the ONDCP Director is provided the specific authority and responsibilities (21 USC 1703 (c)):

- All federal program managers, agency heads, and department heads must submit their drug budget requests to ONDCP at the same time as to their superiors and before transmitting them to OMB.
- The director must certify in writing as to the adequacy of such requests to carry out the objectives of the strategy.
- The director can direct an agency or department to add resources or programs to its budget submission to the OMB.
- ONDCP must approve any reprogramming request of more than $5 million in a drug-control agency's budget and can request reprogramming itself.

COMPILING THE DRUG POLICY

During the past ten years, the process used to compile the federal drug control budget has evolved. The process begins approximately 18 months before the start of each fiscal year. At that time, ONDCP issues its budget guidance to the drug-control agencies. This guidance typically repeats the priorities outlined in the strategy that are relevant to each agency. The issuance of guidance provides a formal vehicle for ONDCP to highlight its budget priorities.

Although the statute requires review of the drug control budget at three stages—program, agency, and department—ONDCP has not required the program-level submission to date.[2] ONDCP thus begins to receive agency-level drug-control budgets in the summer following the issuance of its guidance. ONDCP budget analysts review these submissions in an effort to determine whether they are in accord with the stated goals and objectives of the strategy. For example, if ONDCP has declared an increased emphasis on school-based drug prevention programs, the budget analyst would make sure that ED had requested additional funds for this purpose. In short, ONDCP seeks to match priorities identified in its strategy document with dollar figures reported in the agency budget submissions.

Following this review, the ONDCP Director certifies the adequacy of the budget submissions for carrying out the strategy objectives. The certification takes the form of a letter addressed to the agency. In the more than ten years that ONDCP has been reviewing agency budgets, the director has decertified an agency only once. ONDCP concluded that DOD's submission was inadequate in 1997 (Graham, 1997). DOD and ONDCP subsequently negotiated changes to the request. Although the process has yielded only one instance of outright decertification, ONDCP often uses the threat of decertifying an agency's budget to encourage or coerce changes to its budget submission (Carnevale and Murphy, 1999).

ONDCP repeats the review process at the department level in the autumn. By that time, departments have also submitted their overall requests to OMB. ONDCP's compiling of the federal drug control budget, then, parallels the preparation of the president's annual budget request and the writing of the National Drug Control Strategy. By February of the following year, the president transmits all three documents to Congress.

The result of these efforts is the 200-plus page National Drug Control Strategy Budget Summary, which describes the drug-control activities and the associated resources for each of the agencies.

---

[2]This decision, in part, stems from the fact that it is not entirely clear what constitutes a "program" under the legislation. No governmentwide definition exists, and different agencies interpret the term differently.

THE CHALLENGE OF COUNTING ANTIDRUG DOLLARS

The nature of the antidrug effort, combined with the structure of the federal budget system, significantly complicates the effort to assemble the federal drug control budget. To understand the difficulties these present, it is important to appreciate what that budget is not. It does not represent a congressional appropriation to ONDCP that is then transferred to the other agencies. Almost all the funds are directly requested by, and appropriated to, the agencies.[3] The numbers that constitute the antidrug budget typically do not track neatly with the account or subaccount level data that the Treasury Department and OMB use to plan and monitor governmentwide expenditures. In fact, very few agencies maintain accounts or programs that are considered to be 100-percent dedicated to reducing illicit drug use in the United States. Finally, the effort to reduce the use and consequences of illicit drugs cuts across 12 cabinet-level departments and involves over 50 agencies.

Given these obstacles, what ONDCP presents, as the federal drug budget, is the product of the estimates the various agencies have made of the funds they devote to antidrug efforts (see Murphy, 1994). For a variety of reasons, these estimates are not derived uniformly. First, the agencies have differing institutional histories and represent a broad range of policy areas, including criminal justice, health, and education. Second, the actual work these agencies perform also varies, ranging from the distribution of grants to the actual provision of services. Finally, the agencies have multiple missions, with expenditures on drug-control efforts representing just one of many.

In consultation with ONDCP and OMB, the agencies have developed their own formulas and algorithms to calculate the drug portion of their budgets. For example, a law enforcement agency may estimate that 20 percent of its workload is taken up by antidrug efforts. That agency would then report that its drug budget is 20 percent of its congressional appropriation for the fiscal year.

It should be noted, however, that the development of a drug budget methodology is not merely a mechanical exercise. In some ways,

---

[3]ONDCP does administer the Special Forfeiture Fund, which distributes funds to other agencies, but this program accounts for less than 2 percent of what is represented as the federal drug-control budget.

how an agency chooses to calculate its drug budget is a reflection of how antidrug efforts relate to the agency's overall mission. The above law-enforcement example would suggest that drug-control efforts represent a portion of the activities on which the agency's officers spend time. If the agency were to begin to place a greater emphasis on drug law enforcement through the creation of a special investigative unit, one would expect to see a change in the accounting of resources.

Agencies also exercise discretion in how they calculate drug-control resources. How this discretion is exerted can reflect both political and policy differences.[4] The presence of both alcoholics and illicit drug abusers in treatment programs, for example, raises the issue of how to estimate the antidrug expenditures. Placing the two sets of substance abusers in separate programs would make the accounting task easy. Programmatically, it makes little sense, however, and ignores the fact that many clients abuse both alcohol and illicit drugs. A similar issue arises with regard to estimating the resources directly devoted to reducing illicit drug use as opposed to expenditures that address the various problems related to drug abuse. In these instances the ONDCP budget guidance offers some direction, but considerable room remains for agency interpretation.

The methodologies used to count drug dollars are also the result of partisan and bureaucratic politics. Most were developed in the highly charged political environment of the early 1990s. The problem of illicit drug use had reached something of a zenith on the domestic policy agenda. The Republican Bush administration and ONDCP Director William Bennett were coming under heavy criticism from congressional Democrats for placing too much emphasis on criminal justice (supply reduction) programs. ONDCP's response was to define methodologies that increased expenditures for drug treatment programs.

Agency officials also confront a number of different pressures from within their own organization. Incentives exist to develop a methodology that overstates the resources devoted to drug-control

---

[4]Wildavsky (1966), writing about program budgeting, makes a similar observation. He notes that what administrators choose to include or omit from a program's budget reflects political and policy choices regarding the problem being addressed.

programs. By showing a larger number, for example, the agency could demonstrate its commitment to an important presidential goal without incurring any real cost. Claiming a bigger role in antidrug efforts may also yield strategic leverage in overall budget negotiations. For example, the agency that claims to make a significant contribution to drug-control efforts may have an easier time fending off OMB or congressional cuts to its overall budget than an agency that plays a smaller role in antidrug efforts.

Until recently, there were potential gains to be made by overstating an agency's drug budget and few apparent costs. As ONDCP has begun to assert its authority and play a more active role in managing drug policy, it is conceivable that some agencies will find it advantageous to underreport their antidrug funds. Larger numbers tend to draw more attention. And some of that attention may be unwanted if it takes the form of ONDCP directives.

The challenge of counting drug dollars, then, is essentially an effort to separate out a subset of resources from an organization's total budget. This task is a function of drawing lines between what should be considered "drug control" and what constitutes "everything else." The product of the efforts is the collection of estimates that the president presents to Congress as the federal drug control budget. These estimates are calculated using a variety of methods, involving the exercise of considerable discretion. How that discretion is exercised can also reflect fundamental policy decisions. Refining drug budget methodologies to reflect the antidrug expenditures more accurately is, therefore, more than an accounting exercise.

The drug control budget, then, exists as something of an appendage to the federal government's budget process. Its categories cut across the organizational and functional presentation that both the president and Congress use. This crosscutting nature necessitates using figures based on a variety of calculations. Moreover, because many of these calculations are opaque, it is difficult to determine how much confidence one should place in the figures.

METHODOLOGIES AND THE PURPOSE OF BUDGETS

Raising the issue of the reliability of the drug budget figures in turn raises the question of how much precision and confidence are needed. It would be a waste of time and resources to refine the calculation of these budget figures if there were no apparent need for more accurate numbers.

Budgets serve four purposes: financial control, planning, management, and political advocacy.[5] From a financial control perspective, budgets can be used to track the outlay of dollars to discourage and/or detect waste and abuse. Budgets can also assist managers in assessing performance by providing the costs of inputs associated with particular outputs. Multiyear budgeting facilitates the planning and allocation of resources to pursue long-term policy objectives. Finally, elected officials often use budgets to illustrate commitment to policy choices. Support for a particular position is often accompanied by a call for increased funds. Opponents of a program will seek budget cuts.

The need for precise budget figures varies depending on how administrators intend to use the information. From a control perspective, a great deal of confidence in the budget figures is necessary. Precise numbers are critical to providing an accurate fiscal accounting of funds. Political advocacy anchors the other end of the spectrum in terms of the need for precision. If an official wishes to show support or opposition, the need is only to be able to demonstrate that the budget numbers are moving in the "right" direction. The goals of planning and management fall somewhere in between these two. Clearly, they require greater accuracy than simply demonstrating that a budget number is going up or down, but they do not necessitate being able to track resources down to the last penny.

The history of the drug budget suggests that, in its early incarnations, it was essentially a political document. In the 1970s and through much of the 1980s, the Executive Branch used the figures to demonstrate that it was committing more resources to the problem of illicit drug use (Carnevale and Murphy, 1999). As long as the numbers moved upward, there was little need for or concern about how accurately they reflected the government's programs.

The creation of ONDCP in the late 1980s along with its assigned responsibilities suggest that Congress intended the director to use

---

[5]The first three purposes were identified by Schick (1972a). Political advocacy has been used to describe the use of budget figures as symbols (Murphy, 1994). Rubin (1996) has noted that budgets can be used to prioritize policies beyond the symbolic.

the drug budget certification process to assist in the planning and managing of drug policy. Indeed, lawmakers articulated this vision of the potential effects of these budget powers during confirmation hearings for the first ONDCP Director, William Bennett (U.S. Senate, 1989).

The drug-control budget emerged as a prominent element in the policy debates of the early 1990s. The discussion no longer focused on simply whether the bottom line was getting larger but instead on the distribution of resources across two broad categories: supply reduction (law enforcement) programs and demand reduction (treatment and prevention) programs (see Reuter, 1994). The numbers used to calculate the "supply versus demand" percentage came under greater scrutiny. Lawmakers monitored changes in the ratio of supply-reduction to demand-reduction funds as representative of shifts in policy priorities. There is little evidence to suggest, however, that the budget numbers at the program or agency level received much attention.

Two recent events have placed an even greater emphasis on the role of the drug budget and raised congressional and public expectations regarding ONDCP's ability to plan and manage antidrug efforts. In 1998, Congress included a provision in ONDCP's reauthorization that required agency Inspectors General to "authenticate" a detailed accounting of drug-control resources expended during each fiscal year (PL 105-277, §705(d)). This provision suggests that Congress is seeking some assurance that the drug budget accurately reflects the level of resources devoted to antidrug programs. Also in 1998, ONDCP established a system of performance measures that increased the emphasis placed on accountability (ONDCP, 1998c). Absent confidence in the budget figures, it is difficult to see what utility would exist in writing a strategy document and establishing performance measures, for there would be no way to determine whether sufficient resources were available to support the goals and objectives. The purpose of the drug budget, then, has evolved, suggesting a need for greater confidence in the numbers that comprise it.

The question that emerges, then, is whether the estimates that comprise the federal drug control budget are reliable enough to support ONDCP's management and planning responsibilities. Over ONDCP's 11-year existence, this question has garnered little attention. If the methodologies used to produce the numbers are not appropriate, or if the methodologies are applied in such a way as to produce inaccurate numbers, it is difficult to see the utility in having ONDCP expend the effort it does to review drug budgets. And, perhaps most important, flawed methodologies or their flawed implementation can misrepresent to Congress how the federal government is spending its antidrug resources.

THE ONDCP EXPERIENCE IN A BROADER CONTEXT

ONDCP is not the first policy office to try to estimate the resources devoted to a program that cuts across organizational lines. In fact, this ONDCP effort closely mirrors attempts to institute program budgeting over 30 years ago. Anshen, writing in 1965, argues that

> there is no reason why an effective budget drawn up to assist rational decisionmaking should not identify such activities wherever they occur and permit their aggregation so that both legislators and private citizens can recognize the total size and multiple locations of the identified commitment. (Anshen, 1965, p. 11.)

Drawing on the experience with DOD, program budget advocates argued that a program model would enhance the ability of decisionmakers to identify priorities and better allocate resources among competing claims. Program budgeting's focus on outcomes and objectives also provided a more rational point of departure for budget decisions than an incremental model that began with what was spent in the previous year (Schick, 1972a, pp. 15–40).

Crosscutting programs, such as antipoverty efforts, health research, and foreign aid and development, were cited as prime examples of the types of federal activities that would benefit from a restructured budget presentation (Schick, 1972a, pp. 8–9). Churchman and Schainblatt (1972) even used the state of California's efforts to reduce alcohol abuse as a hypothetical example of how program budgeting might be implemented.

The federal government did begin to initiate program budgeting in the 1960s, but little was done regarding the collection of budget data across agencies. The Bureau of the Budget directed agencies to identify programs within their own organizations, stating that the bureau would "provide leadership in seeking to fit agency program structures into a governmentwide structure." (Bureau of the Budget, 1969.) One way the Bureau of the Budget aggregated some of this budget was in the form of "Special Analyses," tables included in the budget documents the president transmitted to Congress. There is little evidence to suggest that the function of these crosscutting budgets was anything other than political advocacy.

In a relatively short time, the enthusiasm for program budgeting at the federal level waned. Reviews of the experience concluded that the actual influence on decisionmaking was limited and that agency budget officials produced "reams of unsupported, irrelevant justification and description" instead of analysis (Schick, 1972b, p. 97). The identification of programs and allocation of costs became simply a bureaucratic exercise, as opposed to an attempt to plan strategically. Consequently, only DOD, the first federal agency to embrace program budgeting, and the Coast Guard maintained the concept as the foundation of their budgeting approaches.

ONDCP has made the most significant, concerted effort in the federal government since the program budgeting era to collect budget data across organizational lines and use the information to manage a program. The efforts of the Environmental Protection Agency and the Department of Energy to develop crosscutting program budgets for the environment and energy, respectively, did not, in the end, reach far beyond their own agencies.[6] The uniqueness of the ONDCP effort, however, does not render it irrelevant.

Despite the administrative challenges, interest has arisen in defining agency expenditures aimed at addressing the same problem. The federal government's response to terrorism represents one such area. In his annual budget, the president now provides Congress with a description of the contributions of the various agencies to the counterterrorism effort. Most recently, a House subcommittee approved a bill that would establish a national domestic antiterrorism plan as well as coordinate funding for federal programs.[7] A

---

[6]It would seem logical that the Director of Central Intelligence has developed a crosscutting budget for the intelligence community's organizations. Existence of such a budget is only speculation, however, as the information is classified.

[7]The Investigations and Emergency Management Subcommittee of the House Transportation and Infrastructure Committee approved HR 4210, the Coordination of Anti-Terrorism Programs Act, on May 30, 2000.

recent commission that explored ways to combat the proliferation of weapons of mass destruction recommended that a National Director for Combating Proliferation on the National Security Council staff be given responsibility to create a "government-wide database on budget execution of proliferation-related programs" (Commission to Assess the Organization of the Federal Government to Combat the Proliferation of Weapons of Mass Destruction, 1999). Interest has been expressed recently in coordinating funding across programs for issues such as AIDS and the environment.

The realization that the problems the federal government must address do not align neatly into government departments and agencies is not new. ONDCP's effort to estimate the resources devoted to the crosscutting policy area, however, is the most extensive and systematic to date. That level of effort appears appropriate, given how ONDCP uses the drug budget for strategic planning and aims to hold agencies accountable for their performance. Understanding how agencies have approached the task of deriving estimates of their antidrug expenditures and how these processes might be improved should prove useful for ONDCP's efforts to manage federal drug policy. Should interest in the administration of crosscutting programs increase, ONDCP experience will be instructive for those given the responsibility for defining such budgets in the future.

Chapter Three

U.S. COAST GUARD

MISSION

The Coast Guard is a multimission maritime service and one of the nation's five armed forces. Its overarching mission is

> to protect the public, the environment, and U.S. economic interests—in our ports and waterways, along our nation's coast, on international waters, or in any maritime region as required to support national security. (U.S. Coast Guard, 1999c, p. 1.)

Within this definition, the Coast Guard's activities can be divided into three broad functions—enforcement, service, and national defense—as well as into seven specific missions: search and rescue, enforcement of laws and treaties, marine environmental protection, marine safety, aids to navigation, ice operations, and defense readiness.

The Coast Guard is the leading U.S. maritime law-enforcement agency and has broad, multifaceted jurisdictional authority. This translates into the authority to enforce federal law aboard all vessels in waters subject to U.S. jurisdiction and on all vessels subject to U.S. jurisdiction (including U.S.; stateless; and, under certain circumstances, foreign vessels) in international waters. Although the Coast Guard's law-enforcement responsibilities encompass all federal laws and regulations applicable in the maritime realm, priority is given to combating illicit drug traffic, interdicting illegal immigrants at sea, protecting fisheries and living marine resources, ensuring compliance with recreational and other vessel regulations, and responding to vessel incidents involving violent acts or other criminal activity.

The Coast Guard also provides maritime services directly to the American public, including search and rescue, aids to navigation, recreational boating safety, commercial vessel safety, bridge administration, icebreaking services, and marine environmental protection. Finally, the Coast Guard is a military service with mandated national defense and defense readiness responsibilities.

The Coast Guard faces many of the same challenges that the other four military services face: deciding which assets should be deployed for what missions and where. This is not only true among the three broad categories of missions, but also within subsets of the various missions the Coast Guard undertakes. For example, assets used for enforcing laws and treaties must be divided between maritime interdiction of drugs and illegal immigration, as well as enforcement of fishing and economic regulations and treaties. Furthermore, because of the Coast Guard's multimission nature and the necessity to share a set amount of assets, there is a considerable amount of asset "crossover" between the categories. This crossover contributes to the challenges the Coast Guard faces when constructing its budget for the upcoming fiscal year and reporting costs for the various mission areas.

One advantage the Coast Guard has over some other government agencies is its interoperability within its environment of operations. Since the missions the Coast Guard undertakes generally occur in one continuous medium—on the water and at sea, whether on it, over it, or below it—the problems associated with undertaking multiple missions in various environments are minimized. The need for different types of resources is reduced, and there is no organizational "cultural gap" between the broad functions that the Coast Guard serves. Also, because the Coast Guard undertakes a variety of missions, most Coast Guard personnel are comprehensively trained to address all these missions, rather than being specialized to handle one specific mission.

DRUG MISSION

Under the national security heading, the Coast Guard is committed to stemming the drug flow into the United States by "denying smugglers the use of air and maritime routes in the Transit Zone, a six million square mile area, including the Caribbean, Gulf of Mexico and

Eastern Pacific Ocean." (ONDCP, 1998b, p. 166.) The Coast Guard is the lead federal agency for maritime drug interdiction and shares lead responsibility for air interdiction with the U.S. Customs Service. Maritime drug interdiction is an integral part of the National Drug Control Strategy, and these activities clearly contribute to Goal 4 in the ONDCP strategy. The Coast Guard also supports Goal 5 by participating in source-country operations and by engaging and training source and transit nations in order to enhance regional forces' ability to prevent smuggling (U.S. Coast Guard, 1999b, p. 49).

To ensure full alignment with the National Drug Control Strategy's Performance Measures of Effectiveness, the Coast Guard has further defined its Illegal Drug Interdiction Performance Goal in its FY 2000 Performance Plan. This updated plan calls for progressively greater seizure rates and a progressively reduced smuggler success rate by 2002 and on to 2007. This goal focuses on reducing the flow of illegal drugs reaching the United States via noncommercial maritime means.

DRUG BUDGET

The Coast Guard does not have a separate appropriation for drug interdiction activities. Rather, these activities, as well as capital improvements, are funded out of general Coast Guard appropriations.

Understanding the entire Coast Guard budget process is necessary to an understanding of the Coast Guard drug-control budget. The Coast Guard determines its overall budget through an internal allocation of funds to specific projects and mission areas based on prior budgetary data as well as future projections of needs and national goals and priorities in each of its seven missions (search and rescue, enforcement of laws and treaties, marine environmental protection, marine safety, aids to navigation, ice operations, and defense readiness). What differentiates the Coast Guard approach to its drug budget is the use of a cost-allocation model to determine what percentage of costs and resources will be allocated to the drug interdiction mission area.

As Table 3.1 shows, the Coast Guard provides ONDCP with information regarding funding for its drug mission by decision unit: Operat-

Table 3.1

U.S. Coast Guard
FY 1998 Appropriation
(Budget Authority)

Decision Unit	Total Budget[a] ($M)	Drug Budget[b] ($M)	Drug Budget Share of Total (%)
OE	2,714.970	366.128	13.10
AC&I	395.906	34.523	8.54
RDT&E	19.000	0.938	4.20
Total	4,002.494[c]	401.589	10.00

[a]U.S. Coast Guard (1999b).

[b]ONDCP (1998b), p. 165.

[c]U.S. Coast Guard (2000a) p. 28. Since this budget includes categories besides the decision units listed above, the decision unit total does not match the overall total.

ing Expenses (OE); Acquisition, Construction, and Improvements (AC&I); and Research, Development, Test, and Evaluation (RDT&E). In the FY 1998 presentation, the Coast Guard's antidrug efforts represented 10 percent of overall agency funding, with the majority of costs being operating expenses. Each percentage in Table 3.1, however, changes annually based on the Coast Guard's assessment of its ability to continue, at a minimum, its current level of interdiction operations, as well as to meet any new national performance goals. By using an established baseline estimate derived from its cost-allocation methodology (described in the next section), the Coast Guard can assess how much additional funding is necessary to increase interdiction efforts or, conversely, how operating efficiencies can offset reductions in funding.

DRUG BUDGET METHODOLOGY

"Program Budget": The Coast Guard Cost-Allocation Methodology

In the late 1970s, the Coast Guard designed a cost-allocation methodology called Program Budget. Its purpose was systematic quantification of the dollars spent on the Coast Guard's primary missions and programs, which came under the OE account.[1] This methodology allocated Coast Guard costs according to the hours cutters, aircraft, boats, and marine safety personnel spent on various types of missions. Until 1998, operational data (hours of effort) and accounting data were downloaded only at the end of the fiscal year, and budgetary predictions were projected based on this historical data and future incremental changes.

The methodology and software have been updated and can now show quarterly costing in the various mission areas, allowing the Coast Guard to track running costs simultaneously with its budget and to determine where resources should be allocated in the future. The Coast Guard determines the resource hours spent on each of the seven Coast Guard missions by using the Abstract of Operations Report, a traditional military system for logging the hours spent on each particular mission. Using the reported hours logged by commanding officers on ships and by pilots in aircraft, the Coast Guard can determine which of the seven missions Coast Guard personnel and assets have spent their time on. This time-allocation information is combined with financial data gathered from over 3,000 cost centers around the United States to determine the costs associated with each of the seven mission areas

Cost Model Issues

Although the methodology is thorough and precise in terms of tracking resources spent and predicting the necessary future resource expenditures, it does have its limitations. The sheer size and complexity of the cost-allocation model makes it difficult to present a detailed accounting of its drug budget methodology to ONDCP and, in effect, the general public. The Coast Guard maintains detailed records of resource hour expenditures and associated costs, which are used as inputs in its complex cost-allocation model. But this actually contributes to the model's lack of transparency. More specifically, the cost-allocation model does not differentiate between fixed and variable costs in its output, making it necessary for the Coast Guard to find alternative methods for deriving these costs.

---

[1]The OE account is explained in greater detail in the next section.

To address the transparency and cost differentiating issues of the cost-allocation model, the Coast Guard is moving to adopt activity-based costing, management, and budget techniques, which have proven successful in the private sector. The adoption of these accounting methods is also aimed at improving the visibility of the Coast Guard's current opaque cost structure. While this program is still relatively new, initial efforts to incorporate these techniques into the Coast Guard budgeting process have been successful.

DECISION UNIT METHODOLOGIES AND RESOURCE ALLOCATION

The Coast Guard breaks down its drug budget into three decision units: OE, AC&I, and RDT&E. Budget numbers within individual decision units are only estimates of future activity, because the Coast Guard's multiple missions make it impossible to establish with certainty how most Coast Guard assets will be specifically employed. The majority of the funds allocated to the drug budget are found in OE, which involves operating Coast Guard facilities, maintaining capital equipment, and recruiting and training an all-volunteer active-duty military and civilian workforce.

Items contained in the Coast Guard drug-control OE budget reflect drug interdiction's pro rata share of their costs. The share is based on the percentage of time the Coast Guard dedicates aircraft, cutters and boats toward drug interdiction activities. As mentioned previously, the Coast Guard determines the resource hours spent on each of the seven Coast Guard missions by using the Abstract of Operations Report. The costs, which consist primarily of those associated with cutter and helicopter operation hours, are calculated by the cost-allocation model.

AC&I funding, once appropriated, is obligated up to five years hence, making it similar to a multiyear military procurement account. For determining spending on projects in the zero-based AC&I, the Coast Guard determines the percentage of time the new project will contribute to the counterdrug mission based on the percentage of time that the present asset contributed to the drug law-enforcement mission, based on the most recent data available. This percentage, known as the "driver," is used to determine funding allocations for future projects. This percentage is reviewed and updated every year to account for changes in operational concepts. If the new asset does not replace a similar asset, a projection is made to determine what the new asset's drug-related contribution would be as calculated from a five-year baseline.[2]

The final decision unit is RDT&E, which contains funding associated with projects that support the drug mission. An example of this is the test and evaluation of drug detection equipment for improved search techniques under the Comprehensive Maritime Law Enforcement project. RDT&E's cost methodology is similar to that for AC&I.

ANALYSIS

It could be reasonably assumed that the multimission nature of the Coast Guard would limit its ability to track costs precisely and to determine exact percentages of resources spent on each mission. However, this assumption is not applicable to the Coast Guard; rather, by maintaining a system for accurately tracking its operating hours for various missions, the Coast Guard gives itself the necessary flexibility to adjust resource allocations to each mission area as deemed necessary during the fiscal year. This is particularly advantageous to a multimission maritime service that cannot predict with complete certainty what amount of time will be spent on each mission. However, without extensive familiarity with the internal workings of the Coast Guard and its cost-allocation model and budget process, attempting to recreate the Coast Guard's numbers using externally reported data is extremely difficult, if not impossible.

Of the three decision units, AC&I tended to rely the most on using historical data to determine the resources necessary for upcoming projects. While the AC&I account is more straightforward than OE, it also has the least amount of flexibility for adjusting to fluctuations in the budget or ONDCP targets. Like any military procurement budget, the Coast Guard must allocate a proportion of funding over a five-year period for new projects and therefore relies on an appropriation of consistent funding to ensure that the project is executable within the envisioned time frame.

---

[2]The budget baseline provides the Coast Guard with a point of departure in terms of available resource hours for each asset and what the asset is expected to do based on an established threat assessment.

CONCLUSION

The sheer size and volume of the data that go into determining the Coast Guard budget, in addition to the complexity of the cost-allocation model, limit the ability of individuals outside of the Coast Guard to recreate a Coast Guard drug budget. However, given the Coast Guard budget process and how it utilizes its cost-allocation model to project future costs and budget allocations, the Coast Guard has developed and continues to evolve a budgeting methodology that could serve as a model for other law-enforcement agencies in determining their antidrug budgets. Realizing the challenge of describing its approach, the Coast Guard has sought to improve the public presentation of its methodology. The most recent ONDCP drug budget summary, the Coast Guard's drug budget presentation, is easier to understand and more clearly presented (ONDCP, 2000b).

Chapter Four

FEDERAL BUREAU OF PRISONS

MISSION

BOP is an agency within the Department of Justice (DOJ). BOP's overall mission

> is to protect society by confining offenders in the controlled environments of prisons and community-based facilities that are safe, humane, and appropriately secure, and which provide work and other self-improvement opportunities to assist offenders in becoming law-abiding citizens. (BOP, 1999 subsec. III.)

As of September 30, 1999, the bureau maintained 94 institutions housing 133,689 federal inmates. Most of these institutions are BOP-operated facilities, including penitentiaries, federal correctional institutions, federal prison camps, and federal medical centers. About 12 percent of the inmates are incarcerated in contract facilities (community corrections centers and detention facilities) operated by non-BOP staff.[1]

In addition, BOP facilities routinely support the U.S. Marshals Service in housing its prisoners and the INS in detaining sentenced illegal aliens. Finally, BOP incarcerates state and local prisoners under certain circumstances. Notably, the bureau has assumed responsibility for 1,300 sentenced felons in the District of Columbia. The National Capital Revitalization and Self-Government Improvement

---

[1]Derived from notes and discussions with BOP Administration Division, Budget Development Branch.

Act of 1997 mandates that all sentenced felony offenders (approx-imately 8,000) in the District be transferred to BOP facilities by FY 2002.

In 1999, BOP's total inmate population grew by more than 11,000. This was the largest annual increase in BOP's 70-year history. BOP has fought a constant battle to increase its total rated capacity (measured in number of beds by facility) and to reduce overcrowding in its facilities. Despite these efforts, overcrowding increased from 26 to 31 percent in 1999—i.e., there were 31 percent more inmates than the facilities were rated to accommodate.[2]

The bulk of BOP's antidrug mission stems from the portion of its inmate population sentenced for drug-related offenses. The bureau also operates a comprehensive drug treatment program for inmates in correctional facilities and for those released to the community under BOP custody. The drug treatment program has four compo-nents: residential drug abuse program, drug abuse education, non-residential drug abuse counseling, and community transition pro-grams. BOP's mission supports ONDCP Goal 2. Beginning in 1998, the bureau counted its drug treatment program as supporting Goal 3.

BOP reports that about 60 percent of sentenced inmates incarcerated in facilities it operates went to prison for drug-related offenses in the mid- to late 1990s (BOP, 2000).[3] The percentage was significantly lower in the early 1980s but rose sharply over the course of that decade; it has remained relatively stable since. In addition, 30.5 per-cent of the sentenced inmate population meets the criteria for "drug dependence" as defined by the American Psychiatric Association (APA).[4] At any given time, approximately 85 percent of these "drug dependent" inmates actually participate in some facet of the treat-ment program (BOP, 1999, p. 31 of "Salaries and Expenses").

---

[2]Derived from notes and discussions with BOP Administration Division, Budget Development Branch.

[3]This percentage does not include nonsentenced populations (e.g., those in detention centers awaiting trial) or populations in contractor-operated facilities (e.g., "halfway" houses and juvenile detention centers).

[4]Criteria can be found in APA's Diagnostics and Statistical Manual. The percentage is based on ongoing surveys of inmates and has remained relatively constant (APA, 1994).

DRUG BUDGET

The bureau initiates budget formulation by calculating the costs of sustaining current services. Budget analysts adjust these costs by applying three factors: (1) an inflationary factor that DOJ and OMB define; (2) the size and composition of the inmate population projected for the budget year; and (3) annualization of prior-year program increases, as needed. These costs include pay for over 30,000 full-time equivalent positions. This process establishes a "base budget." [5]

The analysts then calculate the costs of new program initiatives such as expanding existing facilities, constructing new facilities, and increasing contract support. BOP's Capacity Planning Committee develops such initiatives using analyses from the BOP Office of Research. The Office of Research analyzes U.S. Court data, prosecution trends, and population projections to project the size and composition of the inmate population—including the size of the drug offender population—in the near and mid terms (e.g., 1–5 years hence). The committee uses the analyses to define the capacity needed to serve the projected population and determines the appropriate mix of new initiative requests. For example, increasing contract beds would serve a rising inmate population in the near term, while new construction would increase capacity 3 to 5 years after appropriation of funds. As construction on new facilities nears completion and as they are prepared for activation, BOP includes attendant operating funds and equipment in its operating budget request.

The operating and capital budgets are divided into six decision units. Salaries and Expenses (S&E) (the activity operating budget) comprises Inmate Care and Programs, Institution Security and Administration, Contract Confinement, and Management and Administration. Buildings and Facilities (the capital budget) comprises New Construction and Modernization and Repair. A seventh unit refers to the drug treatment program and resides within Inmate Care and Pro-

---

[5] Derived from notes and discussions with BOP's Administration Division, Budget Development Branch.

grams, but is reported separately because it is normally funded through the Violent Crime Reduction Trust Fund (VCRTF).[6]

For the most part, there is no separate process by which the drug-related portion of the budget is developed; rather, it is subsumed within the overall agency budget. The notable exception is the drug treatment program. The Violent Crime Control and Law Enforcement Act (VCCLEA) of 1994 requires BOP to treat 100 percent of "eligible" inmates—those with a documented substance abuse problem who are within 24 months of release *and* who volunteer for treatment—in the residential drug abuse program. BOP analysts base the budget request for the drug treatment program on current costs, inflation, projected treatment needs, VCCLEA, and BOP goals.

DRUG BUDGET METHODOLOGY

The ONDCP budget summary states that BOP's "drug control percentages are based on the number of inmates currently incarcerated or projected to be incarcerated for drug convictions." (ONDCP, 1998b.) For inmates with multiple offenses, this number is based on the charges that carry the longest sentences. For example, BOP categorizes an inmate sentenced to six years for drug offenses and three years for weapon offenses as a drug offender but an inmate with the opposite sentences as a weapon offender. Thus, BOP does not include all inmates with drug offenses in its drug-control percentages.

Drug-related budgets for all decision units under S&E and for the Modernization and Repair unit are based on the budget-year percentage of the inmate population sentenced for drug offenses. BOP's budget analysts extract this percentage from a sentencing database called "SENTRY." The Office of Research's projections of future convictions of drug-offenders inform the drug-related budget for New Construction based on expected completion dates. BOP analysts revise the estimates each year and recalculate the drug budget. Thus, for instance, drug-related percentages used in 1996 for programming

---

[6]Savings realized from implementation of the Federal Restructuring Workforce Act of 1994 support the VCRTF. Multiple agencies at the federal, state, and local levels use the funds for both prevention and enforcement.

the FY 1998 budget (62.4 percent) differ from the revised percentages used to report actual spending in FY 1998 (61.4 percent) (ONDCP, 1998b; 1999b).

BOP drug-control budget is computed "after the fact" by applying the percentages to the decision units after the overall agency budget is determined.

The drug treatment program is unique in this regard. Its budget is developed in the same manner as the overall budget—i.e., by establishing a base budget and then adding the costs of any new initiatives. Some parts of the program, notably residential treatment, are voluntary. The court may order others, such as the education program, when sentencing an individual. Thus, requirements for the treatment program are partially based on best estimates of future participation.

ANALYSIS

In the ONDCP budget summary, all agencies present their drug-control resources broken out by goal, function, and decision unit. The presentation by decision unit provides the greatest amount of detail that corresponds to BOP's congressional budget submission. Table 4.1 displays by decision unit the total BOP FY 1998 appropriation, the drug budget as reported by ONDCP, and the drug budget as a percentage of the total appropriation.

Inmate Care and Programs (non-VCRTF) and Institution Security and Administration dominate, together making up 78 percent of the BOP drug budget. The drug treatment program—the VCRTF portion of Inmate Care and Programs—constitutes only about 1 percent.

As shown in Table 4.1, one can easily and directly reconcile the ONDCP-reported BOP drug budget with the Summary Statement and Performance Plan that the agency submits to Congress. Decision units whose budgets are based on budget-year inmate populations are scored as 62-percent drug related. In light of projections that the percentage of the inmate population incarcerated for drug offenses will increase, the new construction unit is scored slightly higher. The VCRTF-funded drug treatment program is scored as 100 percent drug-related. The overall drug-control percentage is 62.4

Table 4.1

Federal Bureau of Prisons
FY 1998 Appropriation
(Budget Authority)

Decision Unit	Total Budget[a] ($M)	Drug Budget[b] ($M)	Drug Budget Share of Total (%)
S&E			
Inmate care and programs (non-VCRTF)	1,062.8	658.9	62.0
Institution security and administration	1,374.4	852.1	62.0
Contract confinement	248.9	154.3	62.0
Management and administration	135.7	84.1	62.0
Buildings and facilities			
New construction	150.9	95.1	63.0
Modernization and repair	104.3	64.6	62.0
Inmate care and programs (VCRTF)	26.1	26.1	100.0
Total	3,102.9	1,935.2	62.4

[a]BOP (1998), "Salaries and Expenses," p. 7, and "Buildings and Facilities," p. 6. Numbers reflect "1998 Appropriations Enacted." Total does not add up due to rounding.
[b]ONDCP (1998b), FY 1998 enacted data. Total does not sum exactly because of rounding.

percent, which matches the number provided in the ONDCP budget summary.

CONCLUSION

In sum, reconciling the BOP drug budget numbers ONDCP reports with the budget numbers that BOP provides to Congress in its Summary Statement and Performance Plan justification document is easy and transparent.

The methodology for determining the BOP drug budget certainly is reasonable. The bureau's *raison d'être* is to provide custodial care for criminal offenders and, being at the tail end of the judicial system, it has no control over its workload. BOP's overall budget thus is derived from the size and character of its inmate population. It seems logical to calculate the drug-related portion of that budget based on the size and character of the part of its population incarcerated for drug offenses.   Moreover, by including in the drug offender category only inmates for whom drug offenses draw the longest sentence, BOP seems to avoid overstating its drug budget. On the other hand, it is reasonable to ask whether the omission of some drug offenders—i.e., those for whom drug offenses do *not* draw the longest sentence—could actually lead to some *under*statement of the BOP drug budget.

Chapter Five

U.S. DEPARTMENT OF DEFENSE

MISSION

DOD's mission is to provide the military forces needed to deter war and to protect the security of the United States (DOD, 2000). This is done through the coordinated efforts of the defense agencies and military services and involves expenditures of over $250 billion (Cohen, 1997, Sec. 3).

Since the enactment of the National Defense Authorization Act in 1989, stemming the flow of drugs into the United States has become a national security priority. DOD is legislatively tasked with three counterdrug responsibilities:

- Be the lead agency for detection and monitoring of aerial and maritime transit of illegal drugs into the United States.

- Integrate the command, control, communications and technical intelligence assets of the federal government dedicated to drug interdiction into an effective communications network.

- Approve and fund the governors' state plans for expanded use of the National Guard in support of drug interdiction and counter-drug activities of domestic law-enforcement agencies.

These activities support the President's International Action Plan, which attempts to

> reduce the flow of illegal drugs into the United States by encouraging reduction in foreign production, combating international traffickers, and reducing demand at home. (ONDCP, 1996a, p. 86.)

DOD maintains a robust counterdrug presence abroad. In its attempt to stem foreign production of illegal drugs, DOD supports comprehensive foreign intelligence collection and analysis programs that assist foreign nations and international and interagency efforts in their attempts to halt, dismantle and arrest drug cartel kingpins and their organizations. Furthermore, DOD is involved in supporting programs that augment the efforts of participating nations to interdict cocaine, perform riverine operations, and provide participating nations' intelligence and assistance in planning on the operational level. DOD maintains extensive maritime air surveillance capabilities in the form of a tracking system and various aircraft and also engages in surveillance operations in various countries. These activities also include supporting law-enforcement agencies that have counterdrug responsibilities.

Domestically, DOD's counterdrug activities are a mix of interdiction and prevention. For domestic interdiction, DOD uses coastal patrol ships in conjunction with air surveillance and cued intelligence to detect the illegal transport of drugs either through the air or on the sea. DOD also directly supports other law-enforcement agencies, such as the U.S. Customs Service, along the southwest border by developing and providing drug detection instruments, trucks, and containers at U.S. ports of entry (ONDCP, 1998b, p. 29).

On the prevention side, DOD's Young Marines and National Guard State Plan programs assist community groups in providing drug prevention and education, focusing on positive role models and drug awareness education for "at risk" youth. Other prevention programs include Drug Education for Youth and Drug Abuse Resistance Education, which consist of a combination of positive mentoring, drug avoidance education, leadership skills, peer-pressure resistance, and counseling services. These programs are provided on military bases in the United States and abroad (ONDCP, 1998b, pp. 28–30).

COUNTERDRUG BUDGET PROCESS

Budget Formulation

There is no separate process for developing the counterdrug budget. Rather, it is defined within the overall budgetary process that produces the annual defense budget. The process itself is broken down into three distinct phases: planning, programming, and budgeting. In the planning phase, the Secretary of Defense, with the advice of the commanders in chief, heads of all agencies, and the military services, provides broad planning and fiscal guidance for the next fiscal year. The Defense Planning Guidance also defines an overall level of DOD spending for the next five-year period, as well as programmatic objectives based on U.S. national security policies and the current world situation. It is within this five-year "top-line" spending plan that the Office of the Secretary of Defense (OSD) defines the approximate size of the DOD counterdrug budget.

In the programmatic phase, the defense agencies, commanders in chief, and military services flesh out the details of their proposed programs and determine how or if the programs they have outlined fit into the funding estimate, using the previous year's spending as the baseline. Each military department relies on the guidance received from OSD; no additional analysis occurs at this level. The end result of these intraservice discussions is a Program Objective Memorandum for each military service, which spells out its programs and proposed funding. These memoranda include counterdrug programs and budgets that are based on the amounts each agency considers necessary for carrying out the counterdrug missions or believes can be allocated to the counterdrug mission given other competing programs. The Program Analysis and Evaluation (PA&E) office evaluates the programs on behalf of the Secretary of Defense and recommends adjustments in the form of Program Decision Memoranda.

In the final budgetary phase, the DOD Comptroller and OMB scrub the programs and make final budget adjustments. The program and budget are then sent to OMB for integration into the president's budget.

In the case of the counterdrug budget, OSD, in conjunction with OMB, conducts the program review. Although PA&E consults closely with OSD's Counterdrug Office, it defers the programmatic adjustments to the DOD Comptroller and OMB. At this point, the ONDCP Director must certify the adequacy of the request in writing or must identify the funding levels that would make the request become adequate. The ONDCP Director also has an opportunity to participate in the president's final review of the overall DOD budget and offer views as to whether the submitted amount is adequate to perform DOD's counterdrug responsibilities.

Counterdrug Budget and Methodology

The ONDCP budget summary breaks out the drug-control resources by goal, function, and decision unit. Counterdrug funding is located in two decision units: the Central Transfer Account (CTA) and the Operational Tempo (OPTEMPO) account of the military departments.

CTA is a line item in the DOD budget and consists of the procurement, operations and maintenance (O&M), personnel, and research and development costs dedicated to the counterdrug effort; it does not include, for the most part, active-duty personnel costs. DOD's reason for omitting personnel costs, defined as "payroll expenses" in the ONDCP budget summary, is that active-duty personnel costs "represent the authorized force structure directly associated with the DOD's National Defense Mission." (ONDCP, 1998b, p. 28.) The personnel costs of the reserve component, however, are included in the counterdrug budget.

According to DOD, the use of CTA allows for rapid programmatic adjustments to address high-priority threats as they develop in its counterdrug efforts. This is a relatively new development, responding to ONDCP's effort to allocate counterdrug resources to its goals. Previously, the decision units were defined in terms of more-specific categories, e.g., dismantling cartels, source nation support, detection and monitoring, law enforcement agency support, and demand reduction.

The other decision unit, OPTEMPO, is a reserve account that is available to cover unforeseen expenses. It provides the individual military departments with the necessary resources to cover unexpected costs related to O&M and procurement, as well as training costs associated with the counterdrug mission, that are not included in CTA. For example, if a plane dedicated to flying surveillance missions in support of the counterdrug operations needs a new engine during the fiscal year, the cost would come out of the OPTEMPO account. Also, since active-duty personal costs are not captured in the CTA portion of the counterdrug budget, service chiefs are requested to allocate a certain amount of funding for active-duty personnel into the OPTEMPO account. Until FY 1994, funding for OPTEMPO was included in CTA. These OPTEMPO funds are an estimate at best, since this account is used for unforeseen costs and expenses.

Table 5.1 shows the breakout of spending by decision unit. CTA has the same four subaccounts found in all DOD budgets: Military Personnel (MILPER), O&M, Procurement, and RDT&E. The counterdrug budget is less than 1 percent of the overall DOD budget. All of the funds in the two decision units are dedicated to the counterdrug effort and are counted as 100 percent in the ONDCP drug budget (ONDCP, 1998b, p. 28).

ANALYSIS

One issue in the DOD counterdrug budget methodology is the failure to include most active-duty personnel costs, while the pay and allowances for reserve component personnel, which includes the National Guard, are included. These reserve personnel costs constitute about 26 percent of the CTA account

Table 5.1

Department of Defense
FY 1998 Appropriation
(Budget Authority)

Decision Unit	Total Budget[a] ($B)	Drug Budget[b] ($B)	Drug Budget Share of Total (%)
CTA			
MILPERS	69.8	0.187	
Operations & maintenance	97.2	0.440	
Procurement	44.8	0.062	
RDT&E	37.1	0.024	
Revolving and management funds	2.6	—	
OPTEMPO		0.135	
Total	251.5	0.848	0.33

SOURCE: DOD (1999), pp. 28–31.

The predictive schedule of reserve personnel and the transparency of the accounts through which funding is allocated make it relatively easy to calculate the costs of those enlisted in the counterdrug mission. However, the constant rotation of personnel to and from the counterdrug mission makes it extremely difficult under the current budgeting system to capture the costs associated with active-duty personnel involved in counterdrug operations. At the same time, some funding for active-duty personnel is included in the OPTEMPO budget. While acceptable to Congress, this method of determining personnel costs does have the effect of underestimating the overall amount in the funding for counterdrug activities in the DOD budget.

The second methodological issue is directly linked to the first. The methodology on the OSD level can account for all dollars spent on the counterdrug mission given the methodological framework under which it operates, i.e., no personnel costs. However, the differences between funding levels ONDCP has determined to be needed to fulfill the counterdrug mission and the funding levels DOD considers to be available for fulfilling the mission are a concern. Most of the spending ONDCP would like DOD to undertake would increase the level of support for existing interdiction or training programs. If the military departments could account for the active-duty personnel costs more accurately than they do now, i.e., using the OPTEMPO account, it could be shown that the majority of the support for these programs is currently in place. Filling in the missing difference might then require only reallocating equipment. In both cases, DOD would be required to examine new accounting methods that could accurately capture active-duty personnel costs. Another small methodological issue is accounting for the funds in the OPTEMPO account. Since the account is an estimate at best, it is inherently difficult to try to determine whether these funds are indeed used toward the counterdrug mission or to determine how much of the funding is used for counterdrug activities.

In the ONDCP FY 1998 budget summary, there was a $20.3 million discrepancy in overall funding between what DOD reported for each goal and what results from adding all the programs up under each specific goal and then totaling these sums. This discrepancy was confirmed to be the result of the several classified programs that are part of the overall DOD counterdrug budget and are not reported publicly.

The CTA system, in use since 1989, is another issue. According to DOD, this system gives them the flexibility to shift resources within the counterdrug budget from one program to another to address high-priority missions or threats. DOD details these resource shifts in the following year's budget submissions to Congress, but they are not highlighted in the ONDCP drug budget summary the following year. Emphasizing this information in the drug budget summary would improve the ability to track the counterdrug missions DOD has given priority and to analyze possible trends in the drug trade.

CONCLUSION

The process, which shapes the DOD counterdrug budget, is a part of the overall defense budget process that takes place each year. DOD's methodology and appropriation are reasonably straightforward. Most importantly, the process gives the ONDCP Director the means to influence the allocation of funds for the counterdrug effort. He introduces his National Drug Strategy Goals into the planning phase, reviews the programs the military services recommend, and has an opportunity to suggest alternative programs and levels of funding before the Secretary of Defense makes his final decisions.

By not including most of the active-duty personnel costs, this budget actually underestimates the overall amount of resources expended on antidrug activities. What that amount is cannot be known without having a methodology for estimating the number of personnel involved. This inability to capture active-duty personnel costs accurately could be causing DOD and ONDCP to underestimate the DOD's counterdrug budget.

Chapter Six

IMMIGRATION AND NATURALIZATION SERVICE

DRUG MISSION

INS' role in the effort to control illicit drugs is part of its enforcement function. At ports of entry, the INS shares with the U.S. Customs Service the responsibility for inspecting individuals, vehicles, and cargo for contraband, including controlled substances. Between ports of entry, the Border Patrol maintains a specific, though overlapping, role in drug interdiction, supporting ONDCP Goal 4.

The ONDCP budget summary identifies two other goals INS programs support.[1] In support of Goal 2, the INS' Detention and Deportation program incarcerates individuals crossing the border illegally who are found to be in possession of drugs. Under this program, the INS also seeks to expedite the deportation of aliens in prisons and jails throughout the country who have been convicted of drug-related crimes (ONDCP, 1998b, p. 122). Goal 5 is the final ONDCP goal the INS supports. The agency's Investigations program pursues and apprehends aliens who commit major criminal offenses. It also interviews and investigates deportable aliens in jails across the country in an effort to gather information on alien organizations involved in drug trafficking (ONDCP, 1998b, p. 122).

DRUG BUDGET METHODOLOGY

ONDCP reported the INS' FY 1998 drug-control appropriation to be just over $400 million. This figure represented 16 percent of the

---

[1]A draft letter from INS Commissioner Doris Meissner to ONDCP Director Barry McCaffrey, identified the agency with only the interdiction goal, Goal 4.

agency's $2.5 billion total budget for that year. To arrive at the $400 million estimate, the INS began by breaking down its budget by decision unit. The funding for each decision unit is multiplied by a percentage intended to represent the relative share of resources devoted to antidrug efforts for that program. The INS uses this method because of the agency's multimission nature.

The 1998 ONDCP budget summary provides a description of the percentages used to calculate the drug-related total of the INS budget.

> The two largest components of the INS drug program, in terms of total resources, are the Border Patrol program and Detention and Deportation program activities. The INS calculates 15 percent of the Border Patrol's and 25 percent of the Detention and Deportation's resources as drug-related. In addition, INS includes resources for Investigations (24 percent), Data and Communications (2 percent), and Research and Development (73 percent) in support of its border and interior enforcement mission. (ONDCP, 1998b, p. 121.)

These percentages have changed little over time. A review of the 1990 ONDCP budget summary (the FY 1991 President's Budget) revealed that ONDCP reported INS drug-control resources were 15 percent of Border Patrol and 29 percent of Detention and Deportation (ONDCP, 1990b, p. 55). The 1992 budget summary was the first to report estimates of 15 and 25 percent, respectively (ONDCP, 1992b, p. 101). The percentages for these two decision units have held constant since then, with some additional decision units being introduced in subsequent years.

The Origins of the Drug Percentages

Basing the drug-related percentages on workload data makes a great deal of sense given the varied activities of the agency. Conversations with current and former budget analysts in several different organizations, however, did not reveal that any data or study formed the basis of these figures. Instead, the budget analysts responsible for the INS at the DOJ, OMB, and ONDCP, in consultation with program officials at INS, constructed the estimates based on their knowledge of the various activities.

Although the appropriate estimates were not agreed upon immediately, the percentages were, in the words of one INS analyst, "locked in" by the early 1990s.[2]

The ONDCP analyst who was responsible for the INS in 1990 did not remember the specific discussions that established the initial percentages. He did, however, find it quite plausible that there were no data to support the figures. He also added that the analysts involved agreed that there would be no alterations to the existing methodology absent a convincing rationale for such a change. Consequently, the percentages have not changed since.

Some exceptions to the application of these percentages do exist. INS analysts noted that the applicable percentages for certain initiatives did not accurately reflect their contribution to drug-control efforts. Therefore, in consultation with ONDCP, they made adjustments on a case-by-case basis.

INS' Integrated Surveillance Intelligence System (ISIS), first proposed in the FY 1998 budget request, illustrates the notion of exceptions to the percentages. The INS intends to use the remote video surveillance technology and sensors of ISIS to observe sections of the land border with Mexico. This equipment would substitute for a Border Patrol officer in a vehicle patrolling a particular section and would act as a force multiplier. For the agency, ISIS is a technological innovation and therefore is counted under Data and Communications. Under the current percentages, 2 percent of the $50 million initiative would be scored as drug related. Since ISIS is designed to augment Border Patrol operations exclusively, the INS scores the system at the Border Patrol rate of 15 percent.

Budget Formulation

The drug-related portion of the INS budget does not feature very prominently as the agency prepares its budget. Instead, it represents

---

[2]Telephone interview with Eric Wolff, April 2, 1999. According to one DOJ budget analyst, the percentages were essentially educated guesses attempting to represent the relative shares of the various decision units devoted to antidrug efforts. These figures were "reasonable" and "ones that everyone could live with." In this case, "everyone" included the analyst himself, INS program officials, the OMB budget examiner who had the INS account, and the ONDCP budget analyst responsible for INS.

an "after-the-fact" series of calculations performed by a senior budget analyst responsible for the ONDCP submission.

From early formulation to enactment by Congress, the budget formulation process can take 18 months. Each spring and into the summer, program officers work with INS budget officials to develop a budget for following fiscal year. The agency submits the total request to OMB in the fall, and it becomes part of the president's budget submitted to Congress the following February. Eventually, Congress will approve some level of resources for the INS as part of the appropriation for the departments of State, Commerce, and Justice for the upcoming fiscal year.

At any time during this process, it is possible to calculate the drug-related portion of the budget by entering numbers into a spreadsheet (assuming that the request does not contain anything meriting special treatment). The INS analyst can enter a request level or congressional mark for a decision unit, apply the relevant percentage, and produce the drug-related amount.

This process is used to prepare the agency's summer submission to ONDCP.[3] Other analysts and program officials contribute to the accompanying narrative. Adjustments for any special initiatives are also made at this time. This submission provides the template for tracking drug-control numbers as the request works its way through the executive branch and legislative process. Once Congress passes a final appropriation bill and the president signs it into law, the INS analyst can estimate the drug-related portion of the budget for that year.

INS officials interviewed noted the advantages of having a relatively simple, consistent, and centralized process for calculating the drug budget numbers. They noted that ONDCP requests for updated figures often had short deadlines and that a more complicated process that involved more people could lead to mistakes. Such a process, they contended, would have examiners spending most of their time explaining why a number changed would limit their ability to focus on the programmatic impacts of the different funding levels.

---

[3]ONDCP's authorizing statute requires agencies to submit drug-related budget requests at the bureau and department levels before submitting the total budget to the OMB (PL 100-690).

Budget Execution

The INS lacks a capacity to track drug-related resources as they are disbursed and expended over the course of a fiscal year. Although the agency does have cost centers that account for different combinations of programs, there are no drug-specific ones. Instead, the INS simply waits for actual expenditure levels to be reported by decision unit, and then the budget analyst applies the same methodology as described above.

RECONCILING BUDGET DOCUMENTS

Although the application of the percentages is relatively straightforward, attempting to reconcile the ONDCP figures with those in the INS congressional submissions is not possible using just these documents. As Table 6.1 illustrates, calculating the drug percentage by combining ONDCP and INS budget submissions yields different figures than those reported in the methodology. Discussions with analysts at the INS and ONDCP revealed that the treatment of Crime Control Act resources accounts for most of the difficulty. Most of the decision units identified as drug related are part of the INS salaries and expenses account. Two other accounts—the Crime Control Act and the Breached Bond Detention Fund, presented as decision units in the ONDCP publication—are separate appropriations accounts for the agency. The Crime Control Act first appeared in the 1996 budget summary. Breached Bond Detention Fund appears for the first time in the 1998 publication.[4]

Comparing the ONDCP documents with the congressional submissions is difficult because, while the INS "spreads" the Crime Control Act funds in each of the program line items, the ONDCP budget summary presents these resources as individual decision units. Reconciling the two different presentations requires knowing how the Crime Control resources in the ONDCP budget summary are distributed among the other decision units.

---

[4]INS officials explained that the fund's authorizing statute (PL 102-395) enables the agency to use these resources for the detention and deportation of aliens (and other activities). Given that significant numbers of the individuals detained or deported have violated U.S. drug laws, these funds are included in the national drug control budget.

Table 6.1

Immigration and Naturalization Service
FY 1998 Appropriation
(Budget Authority)

Decision Unit	Total Budget[a] ($M)	Drug Budget[b] ($M)	Drug Budget Share of Total (%)
Inspections	167.6	23.4	14.0
Border Patrol	877.1	106.3	12.1
Investigations	259.4	58.3	22.5
Intelligence	9.2	2.4	26.1
Detention and deportation	428.3	61.7	14.4
Training	17.3	2.3	13.3
Data and communication	232.9	1.9	0.8
Subtotal	1,991.8	256.3	12.9
Breached Bond Detention Fund	231.0	57.7	25.0
Crime Control Act		86.2	N/A
Other nondrug decision units	278.6	0.0	0.0
Total	2,501.4	400.2	16.0

[a]INS (1998).
[b]ONDCP (1998b), p. 121.

Table 6.2 attempts to reconcile the drug-control budget, combined with the reported drug-related percentages and the spread of the crime control money, to derive a total appropriation.

For most of the decision units, the figures do reconcile. For Border Patrol, there is more variance, which INS analysts explained was a function of special situations. For Data and Communications, the INS separates out the Research and Development portion, which it scores at a higher (73 percent) rate than the remainder of the decision unit. The situation with the Breached Bond Detention Fund is similar to that of as the Crime Control Act. Since almost all the funds are spent on a single decision unit, however, the relationship between this separate account and the drug-control budget is more

Table 6.2

Immigration and Naturalization Service
Reconciling Drug Budget Figures
(Budget Authority)

Decision Unit	Total Budget[a] ($M)	Drug Budget[b] ($M)	Spread of Crime Control Funds ($M)	Total Funds Per Decision Unit ($M)	Derived Drug Share (%)[c]
Inspections	167.6	23.4	1.7	25.1	15.0
Border Patrol	877.1	106.3	31.6	137.9	15.7
Investigation	259.4	58.3	3.9	62.2	24.0
Intelligence	9.2	2.4	0.0	2.4	26.1
Detention and deportation	428.3	61.7	45.3	107.0	25.0
Training	17.3	2.3	0.3	2.6	15.0
Data and communication	232.9	1.9	3.3	5.2	2.2
Subtotal	1,991.8	256.3	86.1	342.4	17.2

[a]INS (1998).

[b]ONDCP (1998b), p. 121.

[c]This column estimates the drug percentage by dividing the total funds per decision unit by the agency budget total.

transparent. The figures submitted to the congressional appropriations subcommittee provide a breakdown of the activities supported by the fund, including $231 million for detention and deportation activities. Using the reported 25 percent that is considered to be drug-related yields the $57.7 million ONDCP reported. The different presentations make it difficult, but not impossible, to track numbers from ONDCP to the agency's congressional budget submissions.

ANALYSIS

INS' Mission Drives the Agency's Drug Role

The description of how the INS calculates the drug portion of its budget provides insight into the role that antidrug efforts play in the agency's overall mission. In short, the drug mission is subsumed in the broader effort and, aside from some special cases, remains relatively indistinguishable from the agency's other enforcement activities.   The agency makes decisions regarding the allocation of resources at the program level, and the effects of these decisions on antidrug efforts are calculated after the fact.

This is not to suggest that program and budget officials do not take the drug mission into consideration. Budget officials claimed that drug law enforcement was a component of discussions regarding the Border Patrol, inspections, and detention resources. The INS Budget Director and the Executive Associate Commissioner for Management also review the drug budget and the submission to ONDCP. But framing resource issues in the context of antidrug activities appears to be the exception rather than the rule at INS. Instead, the calculation and tracking of the INS drug budget seem to be responsive to the reporting requirements and ONDCP inquiries and do not play a major role in the agency's budget process.

Current Drug Percentages Need to Be Updated

Using estimates of the relative workload is an appropriate methodology for a multimission agency, such as the INS. The opportunistic nature of the interdiction task makes it impractical to separate drug law enforcement from the other activities of the Border Patrol, INS inspectors, and INS investigators.

The INS methodology is problematic, however, in that the percentages being used for FY 1998 were derived 7 or 8 years ago and were based on little substantive information. As a result, it is not clear how to interpret the calculated budget numbers. Assuming that the original estimates were accurate *and* that the relative share of the time the INS spends on drug law enforcement has not changed over the period, then the current methodology may produce reasonable estimates of the agency's resources. If the original percentages were flawed or if the relative workload has increased or decreased, however, the FY 1998 budget figures may not be very representative of the true level of resources devoted to antidrug efforts.[5] Since the drug-related percentages have remained constant, the FY 1998 INS

---

[5]Two significant changes have occurred since 1990 that would suggest the relative workload for the Border Patrol may have changed.   First, drug smugglers have increased their use of the U.S.-Mexico border as a transit point for drugs into this country. Second, the Border Patrol has grown dramatically.

drug budget is actually a derivation of estimated 1990–1991 numbers with the workload adjusted upward to reflect growth in the agency's overall budget.

How might the INS update the percentages it uses to calculate the drug-related share of its budget? INS budget officials suggested that the program offices would be best situated to estimate the levels of effort they devote to antidrug activities. They also noted that instituting a recordkeeping system similar to the FBI's might be a good starting point. The FBI's Time Utilization Record-Keeping (TURK) system requires agents to report the number of hours spent on different activities on a daily basis. These logs are then used in estimating the percentage of time agents spend on drug investigations.[6]

How an INS inspector or Border Patrol agent would assign his or her time might prove difficult, given that his or her activities are more reactive than those of an FBI agent. For example, a member of the Border Patrol may spend an eight-hour shift patrolling a section of the U.S.-Mexico land border and not witness any illegal crossings or make any apprehensions. How would that agent account for the time? Arguably, all eight hours were spent looking for drug smugglers. Or, alternately, having the agent assigned to that sector may have deterred drug smugglers from crossing during that shift.

At the other end of the spectrum, one could argue that the only time Border Patrol agents are involved in drug law enforcement is when they make an arrest or seizure. Some back-of-the-envelope calculations suggest such an approach would produce an extremely low estimate of the Border Patrol's workload. For example, in a given year, the Border Patrol may apprehend over 2 million individuals entering the United States illegally. The INS reports that the agency apprehends about 7,000 drug smugglers. Assuming that these are the only apprehensions the Border Patrol makes, drug smugglers represent only 0.35 percent of the workload. Even if the time it takes to apprehend and process a smuggler is 20 times that for an undocumented alien, the share of the workload would only be 7 percent.

---

[6]It is worth noting that, while TURK is a starting point, the FBI does not rely on it entirely when estimating the bureau's drug budget.

Being able to demonstrate that the drug-related percentage of the INS workload may be between 0.35 percent and 100 percent does little to identify the "right" percentage but does reveal the complexity of the issues raised by trying to derive an estimate. At a minimum, the INS could attempt to determine how its inspectors, investigators, and Border Patrol personnel allocate their time. This information would at least provide a historical description of their workload. Making projections regarding the future workload, however, would remain difficult given the nature of the work.

Connection to Performance Tenuous

The purpose for tabulating the federal drug-control budget was to provide some consistent, cross-cutting representation of the level of effort devoted to antidrug activities. As the federal government in general, and ONDCP in particular, begins to increase the emphasis on performance, the budget process could eventually be used to hold agencies accountable for their progress relative to the performance measures. Given current methods for calculating the INS drug budget, the figures do not necessarily represent the agency's level of effort. More importantly, the retrospective approach the INS takes to the drug budget process does not appear to tie antidrug performance to drug-control resources.

CONCLUSION

The methodology used to calculate the drug numbers, though not easily reconstructed, appears to reconcile with the agency's congressional budget submissions. The treatment of the Crime Control Act appropriation and the Breach Bond Detention fund explains much of the difficulty. It also is possible to track the presentation of the budget numbers across the functional, goal, and decision-unit levels.

The most critical question that emerges from this chapter, then, is the degree to which the percentages the INS uses appropriately reflect its level of antidrug effort. The agency uses estimated workload measures to calculate the drug-related portion of resources. This method appears to be a sensible approach and parallels the methodologies that agencies with similar missions use (e.g., the U.S.

Customs Service and the Coast Guard). What is problematic, how-ever, is that the percentages themselves were derived with little sup-porting data to justify them. The actual level of resources devoted to antidrug efforts may be higher or lower than the reported figures, and, even if the percentages represented reasonable estimates of the workload, the INS has not revisited the derivation in at least 7 years. Because the workload percentages may not represent the agency's level of effort, it is difficult to imagine how one would hold the INS accountable for its performance. The current system enables the agency to respond to data requests from ONDCP but has, at best, limited effect on the programs the agency runs.

Chapter Seven

U.S. CUSTOMS SERVICE

MISSION

The overall mission of the U.S. Customs Service "is to ensure that all goods and persons entering and exiting the United States do so in accordance with all United States laws and regulations" (U.S. Customs Service, 1999). The service has a primary statutory responsibility to inspect and process passengers and cargo at U.S. ports of entry. It also shares responsibility with other agencies to monitor and patrol sea lanes and air corridors into the United States. In addition, the Customs Service has broad authority to investigate international financial crime and money laundering, including attempts to funnel proceeds from illegal activities out of the United States. Finally, the Customs Service administers regulations involving the import and export of goods, including assessing and collecting duties and fees on imported merchandise and enforcing provisions of U.S. export control law. The agency operates with over 16,000 full-time equivalent manpower positions, plus some 3,500 reimbursable positions funded with indirect appropriations. Over a third of the directly appropriated positions are inspectors and canine enforcement officers.

The service uses a number of inspection systems at ports of entry to increase the probability of detecting attempts to smuggle contraband into the United States. The agency operates 112 aircraft—including P-3 early warning aircraft, jet interceptors, and helicopters—and a fleet of 87 seagoing vessels. A significant number of additional aircraft and vessels are nonoperational, pending delivery, or on loan to state and local agencies (Customs, 1998, p. USCS O&M-10).

The service's authority to regulate the movement of persons and goods across U.S. borders provides the impetus for its extensive participation in U.S. counterdrug efforts. The agency supports ONDCP Goals 2, 4, and 5. Nearly 80 percent of FY 1998 drug-control funding was reported as dedicated to Goal 4 (ONDCP, 1998b, p. 179).

The Customs Service is divided into 13 offices (each directed by an assistant commissioner) that manage specific activities of the organization, including investigations, field operations, strategic trade, training, and human resource management. In addition, there are four "mission areas"—passenger processing, enforcement, outbound, and trade—each of which is headed by a "process owner." Each process owner maintains representatives in the offices that are relevant to his or her mission area.[1] Thus, the service has a *de facto* matrix structure that encourages views from both within and across functional organizations.[2]

Drug enforcement is scattered throughout this matrix. It is a concern of many of the 13 offices—i.e., it is an activity to which these offices devote some level of effort. Additionally, drug enforcement is considered an important part of the first three mission areas described above; so, drug control is also a focus of the attendant process owners.[3] Thus, for example, the Office of Field Operations, which oversees inspectors, is interested in drug interdiction (both resources available and the results of allocating the resources) at ports of entry. A process owner for the enforcement mission area, which has representatives in the offices of both Field Operations and Investigations (which oversees agents), has a broader view. His interest would straddle the two offices and may include defining the appropriate division of enforcement-related labor between them.

DRUG CONTROL BUDGET

In the ONDCP budget summary, all agencies present their drug-control resources broken out by goal, function, and decision unit.

---

[1]In some cases, an assistant commissioner is also a process owner.

[2]Based on discussions with officials in the Customs Service's Budget Division, March 9, 1999.

[3]The outbound mission area includes efforts to interdict drug money being sent abroad.

The presentation by decision unit provides the greatest amount of detail that corresponds to Customs' congressional budget submission. Table 7.1 displays by decision unit the total Customs FY 1998 appropriation, the drug budget as reported by ONDCP, and the drug budget as a percentage of the total appropriation.

The VCRTF is considered a decision unit in the ONDCP budget summary but a "budget activity" under S&E in the Customs congressional justification document. So, in Table 7.1, the VCRTF appears in brackets to show it as a separate entity even though it is included in the S&E totals. It should be noted that Customs normally uses VCRTF appropriations to buy items with nonrecurring costs—and salaries usually would not fall into this category. The way the VCRTF is reported changes often; while it is part of S&E in FY 1998, it may be reported separately in other years.

The Customs Service receives reimbursable funds from several sources; these drug-related funds are reported separately from the drug-control budget. The agency is reimbursed for its involvement in the Southwest Border High-Intensity Drug Trafficking Area. Customs also receives resources from ONDCP's Special Forfeiture Fund. Part of this fund originates from revenues the departments of Justice and the Treasury generate by seizing property and monetary instruments. Finally, Customs is reimbursed for its participation in intera-

Table 7.1

U.S. Customs Service
FY 1998 Appropriation
(Budget Authority)

Decision Unit	Total Budget[a] ($M)	Drug Budget[b] ($M)	Drug Budget Share of Total (%)
S&E	1,582.8	518.3	32.7
O&M	92.8	88.1	94.9
Harbor maintenance trust fund	3.0	0	0
[VCRTF]	[60.6]	[44.4]	[73.3]
Total	1,678.6	606.4	36.1

[a]U.S Customs Service (1998) p. USCS-1.
[b]ONDCP (1998b), p. 179.

gency crime and drug enforcement task forces. These regional task forces combine the expertise of federal agencies with state and local investigators and prosecutors to target and take down major drug trafficking and money laundering organizations.

ONDCP reports that major Customs initiatives in drug control in FY 1998 included:

- nonintrusive inspection systems ($20.0 million)

- vehicle and container inspection systems ($5.0 million)

- land border port automation ($9.5 million)

- 119 additional cargo inspectors "to conduct intensive narcotics inspections" ($8.4 million)

- forward-looking infrared radars for Customs helicopters ($4.5 million).

The justification document notes only the second, third, and fifth initiatives, which are mentioned in relation to congressional changes to the FY 1998 budget and are funded under the VCRTF. The dollar figures in the budget summary match those in the Customs presentation. According to Customs analysts, the other two initiatives appear in the VCRTF section of the Department of the Treasury's justification document.

DRUG BUDGET METHODOLOGY

There is no separate process for developing the drug-related portion of the budget; rather, drug enforcement is subsumed within the overall agency budget. However, Customs officials maintain that drug enforcement, both as an activity and as a budget focus, retains a high level of visibility within the agency.

Few of the Customs Service's activities are devoted entirely to drug enforcement; rather, Customs focuses on a variety of criminal activities. Additionally, much of the agency's work is "opportunistic"—i.e., criminal elements determine how often, when, and where criminal activity occurs. For example, a Customs inspector has the opportunity to seize illegal narcotics at the U.S.-Mexican border only if a smuggler attempts to cross the border, thereby presenting this opportunity. Thus, it is difficult to account with any precision for the part of the workload that is related to drug enforcement and even more difficult to project future levels of effort. According to the FY 1999 agency submission to ONDCP, "the Customs accounting system currently does not distinguish between drug and other enforcement activities."[4]

Both the FY 1998 and FY 1999 submissions to ONDCP state that Customs bases its drug enforcement resource calculations on a methodology it has applied since 1981 to prepare submissions for the DOJ's "Drug Crosscut" summary tables. The output of this methodology is a set of percentages of total agency resources devoted to drug control that were developed based on expert judgment and are reviewed periodically. Customs officials surmise that the process for formulating drug-related percentages is analogous to an agency process initiated in 1998 to support the president's international crime control strategy. To provide an estimate of its international crime control budget, Customs relied on expert assessments of time or resources recently expended on relevant efforts as part of investigations, passenger and container processing, and other Customs activities.

According to Customs analysts, these percentages generally are used to estimate the resources dedicated to drug enforcement in prior years. The analysts apply the percentages to actual expenditures "after the fact." For current and future years, the agency uses the percentages only to derive a *baseline* drug budget. From this baseline, it appears that the drug budget is refined in the course of formulating the agency budget. According to the ONDCP budget summary,

> in the event a program or budget change impacts a specific area within Customs, programmatic knowledge of the change will be used in determining the exact drug-related impact. (ONDCP, 1998b, p. 180.)

This implies that the methodology is sensitive to instances in which the effects of budget changes on specific programs are known and can be tracked.

---

[4]FY 1999 submission to ONDCP by the U.S. Customs Service, p. 3.

Indeed, as they formulate the agency budget in preparation for its submission to the Department, Customs budget analysts do confer with process owners to base estimates of drug-related funds on assessments of drug-enforcement efforts within their mission areas. The process owners are informed by experts with knowledge of levels of effort being applied to drug enforcement. The budget analysts then adjust the baseline drug budget accordingly to estimate current- and future-year funding levels. The documented percentages therefore do not precisely reflect the actual drug budget in current and future years. Customs officials noted, however, that they have been "close to the mark," despite changes related to programmatic knowledge. Without identifying drug resources directly, "Customs feels the consistent application of the methodology yields a reasonable statement" of the resources (ONDCP, 1998b, p. 180).

Table 7.2 is from the 1998 ONDCP budget summary and breaks down drug-related percentages by decision unit, activity, and subactivity. This is the same table that appears in the FY 1999 Customs submission to ONDCP.[5] The ONDCP budget summary does not identify a total percentage for S&E, but the FY 1999 Customs submission to ONDCP states that it is about 34 percent (Customs, 1998, p. 5). We use this percentage below in our discussion about reconciling FY 1998 budget numbers given inclusion of the table from the same Customs submission.

The ability of Customs analysts to estimate the drug-related share of the budget is hampered by the inconsistency of the information available across different Customs activities. For example, analysts find it easiest to extract antidrug information related to investigations because Customs controls the types of investigations undertaken and hence the level of effort applied to drug control. Moreover, a case management system is in place that captures agents' time by type of case. Knowledge about these cases is used to inform process owners and budget analysts as they develop the Customs budget and determine the share dedicated to drug control. Customs

---

[5]However, there appears to be a mistake in the ONDCP table: "Financial Investigations" is omitted, and "Illegal Export Investigations" is described as 60-percent drug related. In both the FY 1998 and FY 1999 Customs submissions to ONDCP, the former activity has a 60-percent share, and the latter has a 5-percent share.

Table 7.2

U.S. Customs Service Drug Budget Percentages

Decision Unit/ Activity	Subactivity	Drug Enforcement %
S&E		
Inspection and control	Passenger processing	41
	Cargo examination	13
	Canine enforcement	100
	Program support	30
Enforcement	Air interdiction	95
	Marine/other interdiction	95
	Commercial fraud investigations	0
	Financial investigations	60
	Illegal export investigations	5
	Interdiction investigations	100
	Criminal/statutory investigations	25
	Program support	60
	[intelligence]	[50]
	[research and development]	[80]
Tariff and Trade	Appraisal/classification	0
	Regulatory audit	0
	Program support	0
O&M		95
Air facilities and construction		95
VCRTF		100

SOURCE: ONDCP (1998b), p. 179.

does not use the case management system to directly aid in budget development.

Conversely, attaining information about levels of effort in many other Customs activities—such as the use of inspectors for passenger and cargo processing—is much more challenging. These are opportunistic activities that are not subject to choices Customs makes; rather, they depend largely on the levels of contraband or narcotics that appear at the nation's doorstep—the ports of entry. An inspector may engage in drug control in one hour and another activity in the next hour or may engage in several activities simultaneously. Lacking appropriate information—and an adequate system for tracking drug-related levels of effort—Customs analysts are hard pressed to determine drug-control shares within the overall agency budget.

Customs budget analysts employ a methodology similar to the one described above to derive dollars devoted to each of the ONDCP goals. First, they apply the percentages to each of the subactivities to derive the drug-related dollars. Then, they apportion these dollars by subactivity across Goals 2, 4, and 5—again using expert judgment about the share of each subactivity devoted to a specific goal. For example, the Financial Investigations subactivity is 60-percent drug related; 100 percent of that share goes toward meeting Goal 2 (this is the only subactivity devoted to this goal). Numerous subactivities apply to Goals 4 and 5, and analysts and experts deliberate closely to define the applicable percentages. For example, of the 41-percent drug-related share of passenger processing, about 85 percent goes to Goal 4 and the rest to Goal 5.

ANALYSIS

Table 7.3 shows the drug budget as derived using the drug enforcement percentages outlined in the previous section. This derivation indicates a difference of $59.8 million, yielding a Customs drug budget that is about 10 percent higher than the budget identified in the budget summary.

Part of the reason for this is the difference in stated funds associated with the VCRTF, which is portrayed in the ONDCP budget summary as 100 percent drug related. The congressional presentation ascribes $60.6 million to the VCRTF, and the budget summary ascribes $44.4 million. Customs officials noted that they do not consider the VCRTF to be wholly drug-related. The percentage depends upon the programs that the VCRTF is funding in any given year.

Even if we remove the VCRTF from S&E funds, however, a $43.6 million disconnect remains. Overall, the derived figure points to a drug budget that would be nearly 40 percent of the total agency budget, rather than the budget summary's 36 percent.

Table 7.3

U.S. Customs Service
FY 1998 Budget Using Stated Methodology
(Budget Authority)

Decision Unit	Total Budget (Customs) ($M)	Agency Drug Budget (ONDCP) ($M)	Drug Enforcement % (ONDCP)	Derived Drug Budget[a] ($M)
S&E	1,582.8	518.3	34.0[b]	578.1
O&M	92.8	88.1	95.0	88.1
Harbor maintenance trust fund	3.0	0.0	0.0	0.0
[VCRTF]	[60.6]	[44.4]	[100.0]	[60.6]
Total	1,678.6	606.4	39.7	666.2

[a]Derived using percentages stated in the U.S. Customs Service FY 1999 submission to ONDCP and in the ONDCP Budget Summary.

[b]Not provided in the Budget Summary, but stated in the agency submission to ONDCP.

Again, the way we derive this non-VCRTF number for S&E is by applying a percentage (34 percent) that is given in the FY 1999 Customs submission to ONDCP but is absent from the ONDCP budget summary. Reconciling the non-VCRTF discrepancy would require a drug enforcement percentage for S&E of 31 percent. In fact, this is closer to the approximately 30 percent attributed to drug control in the FY 1998 submission. Overall S&E percentages seem to differ in each of the FY 1997–1999 Customs submissions to ONDCP. These differences—between 30 and 34 percent, as stated in the submissions—signify a range of $61 million out of a non-VCRTF S&E total of $473.9 million, or nearly 13 percent.[6]

In sum, one cannot reconcile the budget numbers Customs reports in public documents. To do this, one must have detailed knowledge of the programs in the year being analyzed.

---

[6]Using the FY 1998 non-VCRTF S&E budget of $1,522.2 million, we subtracted the 30-percent figure ($456.6 million) from the 34-percent figure ($517.5 million) to get a difference of $60.9 million. The non-VCRTF total reported by ONDCP is $518.3 million – $44.4 million = $473.9 million.

In general, the drug-related percentages that have been documented and applied to the agency's activities were formulated many years ago and are based on levels of effort prevalent at that time. The percentages have been revisited periodically, and Customs officials have been content to leave them unchanged in most cases. However, the fundamental assumptions underlying these percentages have not been systematically revisited using empirical data. If these assumptions have changed, the percentages may not reflect current levels of effort.

The agency might benefit from exploring options for tracking time expenditures (particularly for inspectors) in ways that could directly aid in budget formulation. One option is to adopt an automated tracking system, but the expense and associated turbulence may be deemed prohibitive. A second, less-expensive option is to sample limited groups of inspectors at regular intervals.

Of course, such options for tracking time would by no means be a panacea. They could only account for some current and historical levels of effort. Given the "opportunistic" nature of its work, the agency would still face the challenges of providing projections. It would also be difficult to separate the time inspectors spend on drug enforcement from that on other activities when they do blind searches of passengers and cargo. The agency might gain insight into this by having inspectors report their time based on a combination of historical levels of effort, location or port of entry, interdiction of narcotics as opposed to other contraband as a share of total confiscations, and intent of searches.

Although Customs documents state that the percentages "have remained basically the same for at least five years," conversations with Customs officials and a review of the stated percentages in different years reveal that the percentages of resources devoted to drug-control activities do, in fact, change (Customs, 1998, p. 3).

From FY 1989 to FY 1992, for example, the Customs drug-control budget was scored at about 45 percent of the total agency budget. Since FY 1993, the percentage has dropped to below 40 percent (to a low of 34 percent in FY 1995). This certainly is related to the removal of the Forfeiture Fund as a decision unit that was scored as entirely devoted to drug control. The "Criminal/Statutory Investigations" subactivity went from 45 percent drug related in the FY 1998 submission to ONDCP (the first year in which the detail embodied in Table 7.2 was provided) to 25 percent in FY 1999; other activities had smaller changes. As previously mentioned, the percentages for S&E ranged from 30 to 34 percent between the FY 1998 and FY 1999 submissions to ONDCP.

The fact that the percentages have changed over the years seems to help soften the possibility that they are outdated. If analysts' efforts to capture programmatic effects influence the percentages, these efforts are beneficial. The main problem involves lack of transparency; without specific knowledge of programmatic changes in a given year, it is difficult to track changes in the drug budget. Moreover, if the documented percentages continue to be based on outdated assumptions, marginal changes to the figures that these percentages produce may still yield numbers far from the actual levels of effort.

The Customs Service applies its drug-related percentages differently depending on whether it is reporting *actual* (last year's), *enacted* (this year's), or *requested* (next year's) budget levels. Customs analysts apply the documented percentages (e.g., those detailed in Table 7.2) to actual budget levels to estimate the drug-control portion of that budget. However, these percentages do not necessarily portray drug-control expenditures in that year accurately, as they may not benefit from detailed knowledge of that year's program. Conversely, these percentages are used only as baselines—supplemented by programmatic knowledge—for deriving the drug-control share of the enacted and requested budgets. Thus, the documented percentages also do not reflect the drug budget in those years accurately. One cannot thereby reconcile the budget numbers in the ONDCP budget summary with those in the agency's congressional justification document.

Although discussions about drug-related performance measures are prominent in the congressional justification document, there appears to be no connection between the drug-control budget and performance. This is not surprising given the nature of the agency's work. The amount of narcotics that the agency seizes and the amount of drug-related money or property it confiscates depend not only on the resources at Customs' disposal but also on the strategies of the smugglers and the organizations that support them. Sudden increases or reductions in confiscations may be based on the decisions of drug-trafficking entities to alter their modes of operation. Conversely, changes in Customs resources may have little effect on meeting certain performance goals, especially in the near term.

CONCLUSION

Reconciling the numbers in the ONDCP budget summary with those in the Customs Service's congressional justification document requires knowledge of programmatic details. From the outside, we have little insight into the actual derivation of the drug enforcement percentages in Table 7.2 (only how they originated) or the drug-related changes made in subactivity funding that altered the stated percentages. As a result, it is difficult to determine whether the drug budget is over- or underestimated and, if so, by how much.

In sum, the methodology used to calculate the drug-control share of the Customs Service budget appears to be a combination of (a) the levels of effort that were prevalent when the percentages were first developed and (b) programmatic knowledge during each budget cycle. This seems a sensible approach for Customs analysts, who have had neither the time nor the resources to initiate an in-depth review of the assumptions behind the documented percentages.

Chapter Eight

FEDERAL BUREAU OF INVESTIGATION

MISSION

The FBI is responsible for investigating violations of all federal laws except those assigned by legislation to other agencies. The FBI's goal is to dismantle criminal organizations. The FBI's antidrug objectives are to identify, disrupt, and dismantle core trafficking organizations. In pursuing its mission, the FBI targets a criminal organization in its entirety, including all its illegal enterprises.

ANTIDRUG ACTIVITIES

The FBI's antidrug activities serve ONDCP Goals 2 and 5. Goal 4 has been part of the FBI's mission but was incorporated into Goal 5 in FY 1998 and reported that way. In subsequent years, it has been broken out separately.[1] Although the FBI is not an interdiction agency like the Coast Guard, Customs, or INS, its activities support these agencies' interdiction objectives. This distinction is important. FBI agents are assigned to particular investigations with particular purposes, including the dismantling of drug-related organized criminal enterprises (OCEs). FBI agents are able to categorize their time as being drug related or as being focused on other activities, and management can assign agents to drug investigations. The interdiction

---

[1]The issue is how Goal 4 is interpreted. Some see protection of the borders as an interdiction function and say the FBI does not do this because it is not an interdiction agency. Others, however, note the FBI's support to law-enforcement activities along the southwest border and state that the bureau supports Goal 4. The bureau captures the funds used for these activities annually and reports them against either Goal 4 or Goal 5.

agencies tend to operate more opportunistically, such as in guarding a border and searching people or containers for many types of illegal activities. Agents engaged in these activities find it more difficult to differentiate between time spent searching for drug traffickers and time spent searching for other smugglers. Thus, it is difficult for management in these opportunistic activities to add resources that focus on the drug problem, since these resources will be applied to all interdiction activities. One result of this difference in activities is seen in performance objectives and measures. Those for the FBI are different from those of the interdiction agencies. For example, the FBI focuses on dismantling organizations; thus, seizures of drugs are not an objective but a by-product of other activities.

ANTIDRUG BUDGET

Table 8.1 shows the distribution of FBI antidrug resources by decision unit. The decision units reflect the bureau's organization and are used to manage its resources.[2] Decision units were first defined in the 1970s and are adjusted as needed based on statutory requirements and criminal activities. All the bureau's decision units contain resources used in the FBI's antidrug mission. Within the decision units there are many subcategories of activities. The subset related to drugs is identified and used as the baseline for developing the bureau's drug budget. Until 1992, the FBI maintained a separate decision unit for drugs, which contained about 60 percent of the bureau's antidrug resources. In 1992, the bureau reorganized and brought drugs into OCE. Additional decision units have been established for administrative purposes. For example, the Crime Control Act listed in the FY 1998 budget is a cross-agency federal program that the FBI administers. Funds for the Organized Crime Drug Enforcement Task Force that were originally appropriated to the 11 agencies involved are now administered through a central, reimbursable, account. ONDCP's budget summary currently reports the task force's requested reimbursements for the next fiscal year but stopped reporting the associated full-time equivalents (FTEs) in FY 1998.

---

[2]The bureau is considering a new resource management structure, which would classify resources according to its strategic plan.

Table 8.1

Federal Bureau of Investigation
FY 1998 Appropriation
(Budget Authority)

Decision Unit	Total Budget[a] ($M)	Drug Budget[b] ($M)	Drug Budget Share of Total (%)
Investigations			
Other field programs	1,179.7	196.6	16.7
OCE	402.5	353.9	88.0
White collar crime	414.3	80.8	19.0
Support			
Training, recruiting, applicant	107.5	11.7	11.0
Forensic services	116.1	24.3	21.0
Information management	145.1	29.6	20.0
Technical field support and services	207.9	20.8	10.0
Criminal justice information services	191.4	41.4	22.0
Management and administration	168.0	25.6	15.0
Crime bill	NA	40.8	
Total S&E	2,932.5	825.5	28.0
Construction	44.5	0.0	0.0
Total	2977.0	825.5	28.0

[a]Enacted figures from DOJ (1998).
[b]ONDCP (1998b).

ONDCP requires the FBI to break out its antidrug resources within each decision unit. The FBI's FY 1998 drug budget was 25 percent of its overall budget. As with the rest of its budget, the biggest portion of the FBI's antidrug resources is assigned to investigations, about 75 percent. The remainder goes to support functions and construction. S&E takes up the largest share of the FBI budget and includes research and development funds. Construction funds are shown separately but amount to less than 1 percent of the budget in FY 1998.

Investigations are classified by the principal violation being pursued (called the *predicate violation*). When that involves a drug violation, the investigation's costs are captured under OCE. However, drug-related crimes also involve other decision units. For example, the drug-related aspects of a money-laundering investigation would fall under White Collar Crime.

FBI ANTIDRUG BUDGET METHODOLOGY

The FY 1997 ONDCP budget summary was the first to describe the FBI's methodology for estimating its antidrug budget. The same methodology was reported in FY 1998.

To formulate outyear budget requests, the FBI begins with the actual FTE data and associated costs from the most recent year for which such information is available (i.e., two years ago). This information is updated once the most recent fiscal year is over. The resulting baseline budget is then adjusted to meet changes in strategic plans, programmatic adjustments, and inflation.

Each decision unit has its own funding for S&E and for major equipment purchases. All research and development projects are funded through Technical Field Support Services.

All field agents in grades 10–13 report their time using a system known as TURK, which includes numerous subcategories for recording the activities of FBI agents, including antidrug activities. Supervisors in the field and management staff do not use this system to report their time. Approximately one-half of the bureau's employees are agents, and about 79 percent of them use the TURK system.

Once the proposed budget is developed, the FBI then determines the proportion involved in antidrug activities. In FY 1998, it used three different methods, depending on the decision unit.

Organized Criminal Enterprises

OCE includes cases for which a drug violation is the predicate violation. Time spent on drug investigations is captured in the TURK system and is used to develop the FBI's antidrug budget. TURK is organized along programmatic lines so that agents working in OCE on antidrug investigations specify their time within an antidrug category. This antidrug time is broken down to capture the antidrug effort more specifically. For example, an agent's time on an antidrug case is categorized by the type of drug-trafficking organization the agent is pursuing and the activity the agent is engaged in. The hours attributed to antidrug activities are added together to determine the number of FTEs expended in antidrug activities. This number of FTEs is next divided by the total FTEs in this division to determine the percentage involved in antidrug activities. This number (88 percent in FY 1998) is then applied to all the OCE costs (S&E as well as equipment purchases) to determine the resources spent on antidrug activities.

White Collar Crimes and the Support Decision Units

Since OCE is the only decision unit focused on dismantling drug-trafficking organizations, there is no antidrug program in the other decision units. This means that, in TURK, these agents cannot allocate their time to antidrug activities even though, in some cases, they will be investigating drug crimes as part of a money laundering or embezzlement investigation. For these decision units, another approach is used to define the resources spent on antidrug activities. For the White Collar Crimes and all the Support decision units (except Technical Field Support and Services), FBI staff identify subcategories of activities in TURK that are potentially drug related. This step is subjective but is based on expert judgment. They then add up the hours, determine the number of FTE, and calculate the costs (salaries and expenses). At this point, the FBI cannot determine what percentage of these costs is drug related. So, analysts use the percentage of FBI investigative FTEs that are OCE FTEs. In FY 1998, this percentage was 19 percent. This percentage was then applied to the costs (salaries and expenses, as well as equipment purchases) in White Collar Crimes and the Support decision units identified as potentially drug related. The resulting costs are reported in the antidrug budgets.

Violent Crimes

The approach used to calculate the White Collar Crimes antidrug costs is also used for Violent Crimes.[3] There is one important difference: The percentage applied to the subset of costs identified as potentially antidrug is based on Bureau of Justice Statistics data on

---

[3]Violent Crimes are included in Other Field Programs.

drug-related violent crime not on the OCE percentage. The number used in FY 1997 was 60 percent.[4]

Technical Services

Research and development projects are found in the Engineering Research Facilities subcategory of Technical Field Support and Services. Since virtually all these projects support multiple missions, the project managers provide the budget office with the portion they judge to support antidrug investigations. The assignment of proportions is based on the expected utility of the technology to the different decision units.

ANALYSIS

Opaque to the Public

The FY 1998 ONDCP budget summary does not accurately reflect the methodology the FBI uses to calculate its antidrug budget. The ONDCP budget summary states that

> the FBI's anti-drug program is a combination of three components: (1) determine the percentage of personnel resources within the Organized Criminal Enterprises that is drug-related and apply that percentage to remaining decision unit resources, (2) calculate a percent of total cost based on crime statistics from the Bureau of Justice Statistics, and (3) direct costs related to drug specific projects. (ONDCP, 1998b, p. 116.)

However, as described by staff and reflected in the budget data presented, the percentage of OCE FTE that is drug related is not directly applied to the other decision units. Otherwise, the antidrug budget would be 88 percent of the overall FBI budget, not the reported 25 percent. Instead, as an intermediate step, OCE antidrug FTE *as a percentage of total FBI field investigative FTE* is calculated.

---

[4]The FBI changed its methodology for Violent Crimes in FY 2001. Within the decision unit, certain TURK categories were identified as drug related. These hours were summed and then divided by the total hours worked on violent crimes. This percentage was then applied to the resources associated with Violent Crimes to yield the Violent Crimes antidrug budget.

In another nuance not described in the ONDCP budget summary, the percentage derived in the intermediate step is applied only after the FBI staff defines the portion of the activities in each decision unit that are potentially drug related.

Although it is not easily replicable, this approach is less arbitrary than a more mathematically based system that might simply assign a percentage to the entire decision unit rather than adjusting for drug related activities.

Methodology Works

In applying the FBI methodology, as explained by FBI staff and using we could, in fact, "reverse-engineer" the FBI's FY 1998 budget requests.[5]

Questionable Methods Used to Calculate Non-OCE Investigations Drug Budget

Although the TURK system could be used to provide antidrug activity timekeeping information for all the investigations decision units, only agents working on drug investigations in OCE were able to allocate their time to drug subcategories in FY 1998.[6] As a result, alternative approaches are used to estimate the proportion of other decision units' resources spent on antidrug activities.

---

[5]The OCE drug FTE number can be estimated using the percentage of the OCE drug budget instead of the total OCE budget. The OCE drug FTE percentage of total FBI investigative FTE can then be calculated using data provided in the FBI budget summary. For the FY 1998 budget request, which is slightly different from the enacted numbers shown in Table 8.1, the OCE FTE percentage of total FBI investigative FTE was 22.5 percent. This is the number the FBI applies against its adjusted S&E for each decision unit, that is, the portion of each decision unit's S&E potentially related to drugs. Thus, this percentage (22.58 percent) should be larger than the percentages calculated as the proportion of each decision unit's *total* budget allocated to drugs. The figures in Table 8.1 are based on the enacted budget but approximate the proportions of the budget request.

[6]The bureau has used the OCE drug FTE percentage of the FBI field investigative FTE to calculate the White Collar Crime and support decision unit drug budgets since at least the early 1990s.

In FY 1998, the amount of violent crime resources allocated to drug control was based on statistics on violent crime provided by the Bureau of Justice Statistics. These data were not adjusted to reflect the proportion of drug-related violent crimes involving the FBI, so the percentage used is likely to be higher than if only federal crimes were included. The FBI changed its approach for FY 2001, resulting in a reduction of $283 million in the violent crimes antidrug budget.

Although it would seem more appropriate, and relatively simple, to establish antidrug TURK categories under White Collar Crimes, the FBI states that it is difficult even for OCE agents to categorize their drug-related activities. Expecting agents working on investigations in which drugs are not a predicate violation to categorize their time as drug related or other accurately is too much. However, the FBI does not explain why using a percentage based on OCE drug-related activities is more accurate than having agents report their time directly. The connection between OCE and White Collar Crime levels of effort is not made in the FBI's description of its drug budget methodology. The link between support decision units and OCE levels of effort is more understandable, since OCE contains the largest portion of the FBI's antidrug activities.

Well over half the bureau's personnel, including support and management staff, do not report their time to TURK. Thus, it is necessary to estimate their drug-control resources. The FBI approach assumes that those who are not agents spend the same time on antidrug activities that agents do. Using the OCE portion of total bureau resources may be the best the bureau can do, given the lack of better data, but OCE does have the largest budget for antidrug activities, which may inflate estimates of the administrative and support costs devoted to antidrug activities.

CONCLUSION

There can be little doubt that the FBI is working hard to accomplish the goals of reducing violent crime and the overseas supply of drugs. Its budgeting approach, as far as it is taken, also appears reasonable, that is, attempting to estimate costs based on the actual hours spent on antidrug investigations. The FBI's two biggest weaknesses are a failure to carry this system through all investigations decision units and a failure to explain adequately the methodology in public documents. If the timekeeping system approach cannot be used across the bureau, a discussion of the reason multiple approaches are used to calculate the antidrug budget would be helpful. Specifically, why is the White Collar Crimes drug budget estimated based on OCE data? Clarification of how the costs of cross-cutting, or multipurpose, activities are allocated would also be useful. Estimating support costs is reasonable, although questions remain about how this methodology is applied. The methodology seems to work best with actual data, raising questions about how the budget estimates submitted to ONDCP are generated since these must be based on budget estimates, not actual expenditures.

Overall, the FBI has a reasonable approach but one that should be carried out more completely and better documented in the ONDCP budget summary. Better documentation will also require better explanations of the accuracy of the estimates and why numbers may not compute exactly as expected based on the methodology.

Chapter Nine

SUBSTANCE ABUSE AND MENTAL HEALTH SERVICES ADMINISTRATION

MISSION

SAMHSA provides substance abuse and mental health services through three centers:

- The Center for Mental Health Services helps speed the application of mental health treatments for patients with mental illness.

- The Center for Substance Abuse Prevention leads federal efforts to prevent alcohol and other drug abuse throughout the United States.

- The Center for Substance Abuse Treatment designs programs to improve treatment services and make them more available to those in need.

In addition, the agency has special offices that coordinate its activities in such specific areas as AIDS, women's services, minority concerns, and managed care.

Most of SAMHSA's work involves federal grants and contracts to state and local agencies and to private service providers. It also supports technical assistance and training programs and maintains data systems structured to collect and disseminate the most current information available in all these areas.

In the federal effort to control illicit drugs, SAMHSA contributes to ONDCP Goals 1 and 3.

DRUG BUDGET METHODOLOGY

This analysis of SAMHSA's antidrug methodology will focus on the FY 1998 budget appropriation by decision unit because this provides the greatest amount of detail (Table 9.1).

Activities 100-Percent Drug Related

SAMHSA has three kinds of Knowledge and Development Application (KDA) programs: mental health, substance abuse prevention, and substance abuse treatment. These programs develop practical knowledge, drawing on theoretical literature as well as findings from controlled trials and other research. Their objective is to transfer this knowledge to practitioners.

Most of the KDA substance abuse treatment and prevention pro- grams focus on activities that include both drugs and alcohol, e.g., helping cities improve treatment, providing services to families. Very few of the programs are limited only to drugs, e.g., Drug Free Com- munities Program, Heroin Treatment programs.

Table 9.1

SAMHSA
FY 1998 Appropriation
(Budget Authority)

Decision Unit	Total Budget ($M)	Drug Budget ($M)	Drug Budget Share of Total (%)
KDA programs			
Mental health	57.964	—	—
Prevention	157.000	157.000	100
Treatment	155.868	155.868	100
Data collection	18.000	18.000	100
SAPPBG	1,310.107	930.400	71
Supp. SAPPBG	50.000	35.500	71
Program management	55.400	22.838	41
Other	393.304	—	—
Total	2,197.643	1,319.606	60

SOURCE: SAMHSA FY 1999, pp. 5, 147, 149; ONDCP (1998b), pp. 66–67.

In their methodology, neither SAMHSA nor ONDCP differentiate between antidrug and other activities but consider the funding for all KDA activities to be 100 percent drug related. So the antidrug budget includes: prevention and treatment programs covering illicit drugs, alcohol, tobacco, and even the abuse of prescription and over the counter drugs.

All of the funding for the Data Collection activities in the Office of Applied Studies (OAS), which focus primarily on the National Household Survey on Drug Abuse, is also included in the antidrug budget.

SAPPBG Programs

SAMHSA collaborates with all U.S. states and territories, as well as other federal agencies, through its Substance Abuse Performance Partnership Block Grants (SAPPBG). These block grants provide for the prevention and treatment of alcohol and other drugs. In contrast to the KDA activities, SAMHSA and ONDCP state that the drug budget includes only the programs that "treat or prevent the use of illegal drugs." But in fact, other programs are included.

SAMHSA and ONDCP Methodology. The way in which SAMHSA and ONDCP allocate funds for the block grants to the antidrug budget is difficult to reconstruct from the methodology that is provided, notwithstanding the detailed description.

PL 102-321, sec. 1921, states that each block grant must spend not less than 35 percent on prevention and treatment activities regarding alcohol and not less than 35 percent on prevention and treatment activities regarding other drugs.

In FY 1996, ONDCP simply stated that approximately 71.1 percent of the current Substance Abuse Block Grant and the new Performance Partnership Grant is considered drug-related. This is based on the current statute, which requires a minimum expenditure for alcohol-only activities (ONDCP, 1996a, p. 128).

ONDCP and SAMHSA described their methodology for assigning SAPPBG funds to the drug budget for the first time in FY 1997. This description of the methodology did not change in FY 1998 and has not changed since then:

Funding the Substance Abuse Performance Partnership Block Grant (SAPPBG) is considered drug-related to the extent that funds are used by the States/Territories for treatment and prevention of the use of illegal drugs and used by the Agency for technical assistance, data collection, and program evaluation. Five percent of the block grant is required to be used for SAMHSA set-aside activities, which support data collection, technical assistance, the National Data Center, and program evaluation. The remaining 95 percent is distributed to the States and Territories where at least: 35 percent must be used for alcohol activities; 35 percent must be used for other drug prevention and treatment activities; and the remaining 30 percent is to be used at the State's discretion, either for alcohol alone, for drugs alone, or shared by both alcohol and drug programs. For budget formulation purposes, SAMHSA and ONDCP agreed to score the discretionary amount equally for alcohol and drugs, with 15 percent assigned to alcohol programs and 15 percent assigned to drug programs. (ONDCP, 1998b, pp. 66–67.)

According to SAMHSA in 1998,

although some set-asides, mandates, and requirements were dropped from the SAPPBG legislation proposed by the Administration for the past two years, SAMHSA has continued to use the same methodology in estimating drug related activities, consistent with the earmarks required by P.L. 102-321. (SAMHSA, FY1999, p. 149.)

In both 1997 and 1998, SAMHSA received a $50 million supplement to the SAPPBG. According to ONDCP and SAMHSA methodology, the mandate for use of these funds was to provide "treatment of the abuse of alcohol and other drugs," and excluded use of any part for SAMHSA set aside activities.

Scoring of the $50 million distribution to the States parallels scoring of the basic SAPPBG, providing treatment support for the abuse of pure alcohol, co-morbid use, and under age twenty-one use, and the abuse of other drugs. (SAMHSA, FY 1999, p. 149.)

The 5 percent of the block grant used for set-aside activities is broken down between prevention and treatment, not between drugs and alcohol. The ONDCP methodology says that these funds should be considered drug related if they are used for "technical assistance, data collection, and program evaluation." That is how they all appear to be used. All are included in the antidrug budget. Some of these activities clearly involve alcohol programs, not just drug programs.

Drug Budget Funding Figures. The SAMHSA and ONDCP methodology described above would yield a funding level for the antidrug budget of $712.806 million. In fact, the ONDCP figure is $965.900 million and includes SAPPBG alcohol treatment programs in which the treatment is primarily for alcohol and secondarily for drugs ($194.190 million), as well as those that serve youth under the age of 21 ($58.904 million). Why?

In the course of preparing the FY 1993 budget, ONDCP wished to raise the percentage of antidrug funding in the block grants, from the existing 50 percent to 70 percent. The office proposed including that part of the alcohol block grants known as comorbidity treatment. No data existed on which to base the funding for these programs. So ONDCP increased the drug budget by an arbitrary 15 percent of the overall SAPPBG appropriation that goes to states and territories. ONDCP also believed that the drug budget should include a portion of the alcohol block grant used to treat youth (under 21) with only alcohol problems, given that such use was illegal. ONDCP used the 1989 National Drug and Alcohol Treatment Unit Survey as a proxy for projecting the amount, which showed that 13 percent of alcoholism clients treated at alcohol and combined facilities were under the age of 21. But, recognizing that the alcohol grants included some comorbidity activities, ONDCP decided to help minimize double counting by including in the drug budget only 13 percent of the grants specified in the 35-percent alcohol grants, or approximately 4 percent of the overall SAPPBG appropriation going to states and territories.

SAMHSA objected, arguing that the minimum spending level required by law for alcohol block grants was 35 percent and that data suggested that there were 2.5 times as many alcohol abusers as drug abusers. SAMHSA preferred using a 65 percent estimate for the drug budget: the 35 percent required by law for drug abuse programs and the entire 30 percent of the block grant available to the states for treatment of either drug or alcohol abuse. SAMHSA was also concerned that no good data existed that could identify the number of people under age 21 who were receiving treatment. The 1989 National Drug and Alcohol Treatment Unit Survey did determine that 12 percent of the clients with an alcohol-only diagnosis were under 21 years of age, but SAMHSA pointed out that this study was not a complete census and that an extrapolation of this data was therefore problematic. OMB sided with ONDCP, and SAMHSA acquiesced (SAMHSA, 1991, 1992).

This then is how SAMHSA and ONDCP assign more than 70 percent of the block grant funds to the antidrug budget (Table 9.2).

Drug Budget Factors. SAMHSA has translated these rules for assigning block grant funds to the antidrug budget into factors or percentages (see Table 9.3). SAMHSA applies these each year to its overall budget to determine the antidrug expenditures, for the presidential budget request, congressional appropriation, and actual spending level. This methodology and the factors have not changed since the FY 1993 budget (SAMHSA, 1991, 1992).

Program Management

According to ONDCP and SAMHSA methodology,

> funding for Program Management activities is considered drug-related to the extent that funds are used to support the operations of the Center for Substance Abuse Treatment (CSAT), the Center for Substance Abuse Prevention (CSAP), and the activities of the Office of Applied Studies (OAS) that are supported by Set-aside funds from the SAPPBG. (SAMHSA, FY 1999, p. 149.)

ONDCP simply states that the program management costs in the antidrug budget totaled $22.838 million, and that 309 FTEs are assigned to Drug Resources. SAMHSA apparently determines these figures by taking what was actually spent in the previous year in each of the centers and offices, then assigning them a pro rata share of the budget for the next fiscal year. The only question that arises is why OAS program funds are included in the antidrug budget but not the program management funds of the OAS Data Collection Activities.

ONDCP Goals

SAMHSA programs contribute to ONDCP Goals 1 and 3. For Goal 1, SAMHSA includes the KDA substance abuse prevention programs,

Table 9.2

SAMHSA Methodology
(Budget Authority)

	Substance Abuse Block Grants ($M)	SSI Supplement[a] ($M)	Total Drug Budget ($M)
Appropriation	1,310.107	50.000	
Set-aside (5%)	65.505		65.505
Grants to states	1,244.602	50.000	
Drug grants (50%)[b]	622.301	25.000	647.301
Drug Funds			**712.806**
Alcohol comorbidity	186.690	7.500	194.190
Under-21	56.597	2.308	58.905
Drug budget			**965.901**

SOURCE: See SAMHSA (FY 1999), pp. 5, 147, 149, and ONDCP (1998b), pp. 66–67. Figures are rounded.

[a]SAMHSA (FY 1999), p. 135. Five percent of the SAPPBG funds is required to be used for set-aside activities that support data collection, etc. SAPPBG supplemental funds cannot be used for set aside activities.

[b]The methodology states that 35 percent must be used for drug prevention, and the discretionary amount of 30 percent is scored equally, with 15 percent for drugs.

Table 9.3

Budget Factors for SAMHSA Budget

	Factor (%)
Set-aside	5.000
Pure alcohol	28.930
Drug prevention	9.500
Drug treatment	35.625
State admin (treatment)	2.375
Comorbid use	14.250
Under 21	4.320
Total	100.000

the block grant funds for prevention (the set aside, drug, and program management funds) plus 20 percent of the comorbid and under-21 funds, for a total of $375.5 million.

SAMHSA calculates funding for Goal 3 by including the KDA treatment funds, the block-grant treatment funds (the set-aside, drug, and program management funds) plus 80 percent of the comorbid and under-21 funds, for a total of $944.1 million. All the KDA substance abuse treatment programs, which include alcohol and tobacco programs, are assigned to ONDCP's Goal 3, even though ONDCP's description says that this goal focuses only on drugs.

CONCLUSION

Neither SAMHSA nor ONDCP present clearly how they allocate funds to the SAMHSA antidrug budget. If the methodology that SAMHSA and ONDCP present were simply applied, the SAMHSA antidrug budget would be significantly less, some 20 percent or $250 million less. The actual percentages used to define the antidrug budget have not been disclosed. The inflated figure for the antidrug budget includes treatment and prevention programs focused primarily on alcohol abuse.

The methodology is based on a set of essentially arbitrary rules and assumptions, which were defined in 1992 and have not changed. It is not based on any empirical data or derived from how any of the funds have actually been spent at any time in the past. SAMHSA receives some information from the grantees, but SAMHSA officials argue that it does not provide them with the means to determine whether the funds are spent on drug or alcohol programs. And, because the organizations receiving these federal grants are also receiving grants from other sources (state and local governments and private organizations), it is difficult for them to separate out how the federal funds are being spent.

In summary, the antidrug budget figures do not provide a description of what is actually being spent on drug programs. Rather, they give a rough measure of the trends over the past decade in overall SAMHSA spending on substance abuse programs.

Chapter Ten

DEPARTMENT OF VETERANS AFFAIRS

MISSION

DVA provides a wide range of services to veterans, including medical care, compensation, pensions, education assistance, vocational rehabilitation (VR) and counseling, loan guarantees, insurance, and burial. Services are provided through a number of facilities spread around the country as well from headquarters in Washington. The department has an annual budget of over $42 billion. In FY 1998 over 40 percent of the department's budget was allocated to medical care, of which about 6 percent was spent on drug abuse treatment and prevention. Overall, 2.6 percent of the department's budget was allocated to the drug-control mission.

The department's drug mission is treatment, with the drug budget allocated entirely to Goal 3 (ONDCP, 1998c, App. B). The department also plays a minor reporting role to support Goal 1, Objective 10 (support and highlight research, including the development of scientific information to inform drug, alcohol, and tobacco prevention programs targeting young Americans). The department is part of an interagency working group measuring the impact of education initiatives on drug use prevalence.

DRUG BUDGET

The department's drug budget is allocated to three functional areas: prevention, medical research, and treatment. However, there are only two decision units: Medical Care, which includes both prevention and treatment, and Medical Research. Table 10.1 shows the

Table 10.1

Department of Veterans Affairs
FY 1998 Appropriation
(Budget Authority)

	Total Budget[a] ($M)	Drug Budget[b] ($M)	Drug Budget Share of Total (%)
Medical care	17,745.091	1,092.632	6.1
(drug prevention)		(0.341)	
(drug treatment)		(1,092.291)	
Medical research	272.000	4.570	1.7
Other	24,722.586		
Total	42,739.677	1,097.202	2.6

[a]DVA (1998), Vol. V, p. 2-63. The drug-control budget is not reported separately.
[b]ONDCP (1998b), p. 204.

appropriation for FY 1998 as reported in the department's FY 1999 budget submission and ONDCP's FY 1998 budget summary.

MEDICAL RESEARCH DECISION UNIT

The department relies on investigator-initiated research to form its research agenda. Proposals are submitted in all areas of medical science, and federally chartered merit review boards review and score the applications. Recommendations from the boards go to the directors of various research services and, on occasion, to the Chief Research and Development Officer for final approval. In choosing among research proposals, the directors consider the scientific recommendations of the review boards, the department's program needs, and the availability of funds. Once the research agenda is set, projects having to do with drug-abuse prevention and treatment are identified and reported as part of the department's drug budget.

MEDICAL CARE DECISION UNIT

Drug Prevention

The department's prevention program is focused on drug testing of employees, and the costs, which are incurred by the Navy contractor, are reported in the prevention part of the drug-control budget. Considerable detail on these costs is provided in the budget request submitted to ONDCP. Staff time spent running the program is not allocated to drug control, because the department estimates that it takes existing staff no more than 25 percent of their time.

Drug Treatment

The largest part of the department's drug-control budget is treatment. It has two treatment categories: Specialized Drug Treatment and Other Related Treatment.

Specialized Drug Treatment. The department has three kinds of substance-abuse programs: specific drug abuse, more-general substance-abuse, and specific alcohol-abuse programs. Specialized drug treatment includes both specific drug programs and general substance-abuse programs. The DVA notes that the majority of drug abuse patients are treated through the broader substance-abuse programs because most drug abusers also abuse other substances such as alcohol. The department defines its Specialized Drug Treatment budget using empirical data on patient diagnoses and costs. The FY 1998 budget was built using data from FY 1995.

Staff at the department's Program Evaluation and Resources Center (PERC) in Palo Alto use diagnostic data from the department's Austin Automation Center to identify the patients in each of the substance-abuse programs. This information is reliably collected for inpatients and domiciliary patients, whose records contain diagnosis codes. Before 1998, diagnosis codes were not used for outpatients, so other estimating techniques were used to derive these numbers.[1] The

---

[1]As a first approximation, patient records are searched to see whether the outpatients have had inpatient or domiciliary care and, if so, whether there is an associated drug diagnosis. If so, these outpatients are designated as drug-treatment patients. The number of visits and the types of clinics are also examined. Outpatients of methadone clinics are getting drug treatment, and other outpatients with 180 or more visits to clinics are also assumed to be getting such treatment. Outpatients are assigned weighted factors that are based on such indicators as the certainty of knowledge about their drug treatment. For example, those with drug abuse diagnoses and those visiting designated methadone clinics are weighted more heavily than those who had 180 visits to clinics, which are assumed to be for methadone but might not be. In all, eight categories of outpatient drug treatment indicating different levels of certainty about whether the individual had drug treatment are used. These weighted factors are consolidated into one factor, a percentage, which is provided to headquarters.

recent introduction of outpatient diagnosis codes should provide the department with better data on the portion of outpatients receiving drug treatment.

After analyzing diagnostic data on substance-abuse patients, PERC provides headquarters budget staff with the percentage of patients in specialized drug treatment programs. The percentages for 1997 appear in Table 10.2

The Austin Automation Center collects the costs for all substance-abuse programs in DVA treatment facilities. These costs are arranged in standard DVA accounting codes and are presented in the same categories PERC uses: inpatient, outpatient, and domiciliary. Although there is a DVA handbook explaining how facilities should allocate costs, Austin Automation Center analysts report that different practices exist among and within facilities. They noted, however, that a new data support system is being designed to improve the accuracy and fidelity of the department's cost data.

The department multiplies the costs of the substance-abuse programs by the percentage of patients in specialized drug-treatment programs to calculate the Specialized Drug Treatment budget for the past year. Estimates for future years adjust the substance-abuse program costs for inflation, then apply the same percentage. According to the ONDCP budget summary and the budget information that DVA provided to ONDCP, 62.9 percent of substance-abuse patients are being treated for drug abuse. This percentage was developed in the early 1990s based on a survey of the inpatient population. Although PERC calculates the percentages annually that the budget analysts use, the historical percentage continues to appear in descriptions of budget methodologies.[2]

Other Related Treatment. Drug abuse patients may also receive other medical treatment. Staff at PERC collect data on their other medical care, in terms of the number of days and the category (domiciliary, inpatient, or outpatient). Headquarters staff provide PERC with per diem rates for each of these three categories of care.[3]

---

[2]The FY 2001 budget summary shows a new percentage, 78 percent.

[3]The per diem rates for inpatients vary depending on the type of unit in which treatment occurs.

Table 10.2

**Patients in Drug Treatment
Programs in 1997 (%)**

Inpatient	69.01
Domiciliary	71.76
Outpatient	78.40

The percentages are reported in Table 10.2 and were originally agreed upon in the early 1990s. The costs of this care are allocated, in whole or in part, to the drug budget depending on the patient's drug-abuse diagnosis.

For example, an addict might be placed in a substance-abuse unit after an accident but also receive treatment over a number of days for a broken bone. But 100 percent of the costs of the care for the broken bone would be included in the other related costs category of the drug budget. For patients not housed in substance- or drug-abuse units, the proportion of other medical costs included varies according to their drug diagnosis. It would be 100 percent for those with a primary drug diagnosis, 50 percent for a secondary diagnosis, and 25 percent for an associated diagnosis (ONDCP, 1998b, pp. 204–205). Some patients diagnosed with drug-abuse problems decline any drug treatment, but their other related costs are still treated as drug related.

The budget for these other related medical costs is significantly more than that for drug abuse treatment, and represents over 60 percent of the department's overall drug budget. Table 10.3 shows the funding for FY 1997, which is the most recent year for which actual data is available.

CONCLUSION

DVA's methodology uses empirical data on patient diagnoses and medical care treatment costs.[4] These data are broken out according to the type of care (inpatient, outpatient, and domiciliary). Past

---

[4]RAND has not reviewed these data and thus cannot verify their accuracy.

deficiencies in the coding of information on outpatients and in the costing data support system are being remedied.

Problems arise in the ways that this methodology is presented publicly. There is little transparency in how the department calculates the patients and costs in various programs. The costs for specialized drug treatment and other related care are not distinguished. Some of the percentages being used are not those described. Others being used were defined in the early 1990s and have not changed.

More importantly, over 60 percent of the department's overall drug budget goes for medical care that is not directly related to antidrug prevention or treatment. By comparison, HCFA, another federal agency providing drug treatment as part of its medical care mission, does not include other related medical care costs in its drug-control budget. At the direction of ONDCP, the department does not count costs for patients treated in specific alcohol-abuse programs, only those for patients being treated for both drug and alcohol abuse.

Basing budget estimates on the number of patients and costs from previous years is a useful starting point. But the methodology has lacked any effort to predict future demands on the drug treatment program. The same number of patients is anticipated each year. Changes in veterans' demographics and the department's policies could be expected to affect the drug budget. The budget documents note various efforts to track trends but state that not enough information is currently available to assess their budgetary effects.

Table 10.3

Department of Veterans Affairs
FY 1997 Appropriation
(Budget Authority)

Decision Unit	Drug Budget ($M)	Share of Drug Budget (%)
Medical research	4.400	0.40
Drug abuse prevention	0.181	0.02
Specialized drug treatment	363.020	33.69
Other related treatment	710.010	65.89
Total	1,077.611	100.00

SOURCE: Data provided by DVA budget staff.

Chapter Eleven

HEALTH CARE FINANCING ADMINISTRATION

MISSION

HCFA administers Medicare, Medicaid, the Children's Health Insurance Program (CHIP), and a fraud prevention program. Medicare is the federal health insurance program for people age 65 or older and people under age 65 who are disabled or suffer from end-stage renal disease. Medicare has two parts. Part A is hospital insurance plus some additional related care, including hospice care. Part B pays for outpatient care, some equipment, home health care, and other similar services and supplies. Medicaid provides grants to states for the inpatient and outpatient medical care of low-income individuals. Although the states administer Medicaid, its costs are split, with the states paying 44 percent of the costs and the federal government picking up the remaining 56 percent. The Balanced Budget Act of 1997 established the CHIP to provide funding to states to purchase health care coverage for low-income, uninsured children.

ANTIDRUG ACTIVITIES

HCFA's antidrug activities are the financial support it provides through Medicare and Medicaid to people seeking treatment for drug abuse problems.[1] All HCFA funds are allocated to ONDCP Goal 3. Table 11.1 shows the distribution of antidrug resources by decision unit.

---

[1]Some children in the new CHIP may also need drug treatment; however, the ONDCP budget summary does not discuss these potential costs.

Table 11.1

Health Care Financing Administration
FY 1998 Appropriation
(Budget Authority)

	Total Budget[a] ($M)	Drug Budget[b] ($M)	Drug Budget Share of Total (%)
Medicaid (federal) share	100,960	290	0.29
Medicare (Part A)	198,041	70	0.04
Total	299,001[c]	360	0.10

[a]HCFA (1998) for enacted budget.

[b]ONDCP (1998b).

[c]Total derived from HCFA data shown here is $3.564 billion less than the HCFA total shown in the ONDCP budget book. Analysts at HCFA validated the numbers reported by them and we do not know what accounts for the $3.6 billion difference. However, $3.6 billion is only one percent of the HCFA budget.

Analysis of the budget data shows that, in nominal dollars, the HCFA drug treatment budget has tripled since 1989, from $140 million to $450 million. The greatest share of the increase came from Medicaid, which rose threefold, while Medicare drug treatment expenses rose by only 80 percent over the same period. Medicaid's share of HCFA's antidrug budget rose from 71 percent in 1990 to 81 percent in 1998. During the same period, Medicare's share of HCFA's antidrug budget fell from 29 percent to 19 percent.

ANTIDRUG BUDGET METHODOLOGY

HCFA's antidrug budget captures two sets of drug treatment costs. Those associated with Medicare (Part A), which are hospital costs, and those associated with both hospital and nonhospital Medicaid treatment. HCFA's antidrug budget methodology was developed in 1989 and is documented in an internal memo (HCFA, 1989). In making its initial estimates, HCFA attempted to exclude treatment for alcohol abuse, focusing the estimates solely on treatment for drug abuse. In addition, the decision was made to exclude the costs of treatment indirectly related to drug abuse. This was done because of the perceived difficulty in determining whether illnesses or injuries were related to drug use or were simply happening to patients with drug abuse diagnoses.

Medicare

The Medicare budget is based on inpatient diagnosis data maintained by the Medicare program.[2] Estimates of the number of patients receiving drug treatment and the costs associated with this treatment were made in 1990. These estimates have been inflated annually based on standard inflation rates for medical costs Medicare uses, with additional adjustments made to reflect expected increases in the number of patients. Medicare (Part B) costs have not been included because no diagnosis codes existed to capture drug-treatment costs for outpatient treatment. These Part B expenses are thought to be significantly smaller than the Part A drug-treatment expenses. Medicare recently began using diagnosis codes for outpatient care, so it may be possible in the future to estimate drug-treatment costs for outpatients.

Medicaid

Medicaid inpatient drug-treatment budget estimates are based on 1983 data from the National Hospital Discharge Survey. HCFA used these data to estimate the number and cost of drug-related hospital visits of Medicaid recipients. These data have been adjusted each year for inflation and for anticipated increases in patient load. Because the federal government pays only a portion of these Medicaid costs, and the states pay the rest, these estimated total costs are adjusted by the Federal Medical Assistance Percentage, which is 56 percent. Only the federal numbers are reported to ONDCP.

The Medicaid outpatient drug-treatment budget is also based on data collected in the 1980s. HCFA used the National Institute on Drug Abuse's 1988 Household Survey on Drug Abuse data to estimate the number of illicit drug users on Medicaid. It used 1987 data from the National Institute on Drug Abuse and the National Institute on Alcohol Abuse and Alcoholism that reported total annual clients

---

[2]Data used are from the Medicare Provider Analysis and Review file and the National Drug and Alcoholism Treatment Unit Survey.

and costs funded by public third-party payers (Medicaid and others) to estimate the proportion of Medicaid drug users who might have sought outpatient treatment and to estimate the costs of their treatment. These estimates have been adjusted since 1989 to account for projected increases in patient load and inflation in medical care costs. The Federal Medical Assistance Percentage is used to derive the outpatient portion of HCFA's Medicaid drug-treatment budget for ONDCP.

CONCLUSION

HCFA's drug-treatment budget is less than 1 percent of the agency's total budget. It has not been a topic of interest externally and is not large enough to be the focus of significant internal effort or debate. When asked to estimate a drug-treatment budget in 1989, HCFA engaged in a modest effort to estimate numbers of patients and associated costs. These estimates served as the program baseline in subsequent years. The baseline figures were adjusted for medical-care cost inflation and for additional perceived or expected increases in the number of patients receiving drug treatment. The FY 1998 ONDCP budget summary reports that Medicare Part A budgets increased substantially that year as a result of revised analysis of a 1990 survey. In addition, the Medicare Part A request increased substantially because of an increase in the numbers of Medicare-eligible people requiring drug-abuse treatment. More information on the survey and reasons for revising the analysis would be helpful.

A review of annual changes in the Medicare and Medicaid drug budget over the past decade shows dramatic increases and decreases in the Medicare portion. This suggests that a methodology has been used that differs from the simple adjustment process that the staff described. A more rigorous accounting of the budget-adjustment process used to generate the annual antidrug treatment budget seems to be in order.

The decision not to include Medicare Part B could substantially understate the budget if significant numbers of patients over 65 participate in outpatient drug-treatment programs. The Veterans Administration tends to provide more of its drug treatment care in such settings, so it would seem to be important to provide at least an estimate of the drug treatment costs not being captured in the HCFA antidrug budget.

The ONDCP budget summary for HCFA notes that, under Medicaid, the costs for people aged 22 to 64 being treated in institutions for mental diseases are excluded. This applies to all their treatment costs, not just the costs for drug treatment. The costs of these patients are borne by the states, so any associated drug treatment costs are not visible to, nor managed by, HCFA. This exclusion is not a methodological issue for HCFA's antidrug budget but is important to those seeking to understand public spending on drug treatment.

HCFA's antidrug budget estimates rely on a 1989 baseline updated with 1990 data. It is likely that improvements in database management and other process changes would allow HCFA to improve on these estimates, should it choose to spend the resources to do so. While some undercounting undoubtedly occurs because of the exclusion of Medicare Part B patients, these may be compensated for by adjusting for perceived, but undocumented, increases in the demand for drug treatment among the included segments of the patient population.

Chapter Twelve

U.S. DEPARTMENT OF EDUCATION

DRUG MISSION

ED's overall mission is to provide research, technical, and financial support to educational institutions and students. The department's programs serve the entire educational spectrum, from preschool; through primary and secondary education; to vocational, college, and university settings. It is within this context that ED administers programs designed to reduce the use of illicit drugs by young people and to mitigate the consequences of that use. The department's programs fall into the two broad categories of drug prevention and support for drug treatment services.

ED's largest antidrug activity is the Safe and Drug-Free Schools and Communities (SDFSC) grant program. The SDFSC program supports ONDCP's Goal 1. Congress originally established the program as the Drug-Free Schools and Communities Act as part of the Antidrug Abuse Act of 1986 (PL 100-690). This formula grant distributed funds to state and local education agencies for drug prevention activities.

As its current title suggests, the program has been modified during the reauthorization process. Title IV of the Elementary and Secondary Education Act was amended in 1994 to change the name of the program to include the word "safe" and to expand its scope. Beginning in FY 1995, the program included activities to prevent school violence and to address school discipline issues, as well as to prevent drug use (ONDCP, 1994b, p. 28).

In addition to the grants distributed to the states, the SDFSC program also contains a National Programs component. The department uses the National Programs resources to fund the development of new drug and violence prevention programs and materials; program evaluations; and, if necessary, direct services to schools with severe drug and violence problems.[1]

ED also administers a number of programs that support ONDCP Goal 3. From a functional perspective, ONDCP identifies these programs as treatment or treatment research.

Grants to states for VR constitute the largest share of the reported drug treatment resources. The VR grants provide counseling and training to disabled individuals to prepare them for employment. Some of the individuals receiving these services are drug dependent.

The Special Education programs (Grants for Infants and Families and National Activities) provide resources to assist children with disabilities. These funds are used to identify and serve infants and toddlers prenatally exposed to illicit drugs. The department distributes the funds to the states on a formula basis, as well as through a competitive grant application process. FY 1998, however, was the last year that these programs were included in the federal drug-control budget.

ED funds treatment research as part of its National Institute on Disability and Rehabilitation Research (NIDRR) program. This program supports research designed to assist disabled individuals to integrate into the workforce and society.

DRUG BUDGET METHODOLOGY

For FY 1998, ED reported $685 million in drug-control expenditures (Table 12.1). The department uses three different methods to calculate the share of its budget devoted to antidrug activities. In one instance, it considers the entire program to represent drug-control resources. For other programs, the department counts a portion of the funds as drug related, based on estimates of the characteristics of the clients receiving services. For certain decision units, ED attempts to identify individual items within a broader category and scores them as drug-control resources.

---

[1] Elementary and Secondary Education Act of 1994, Title IV, §4121, subpart 2, Part A.

Table 12.1

Department of Education
FY 1998 Appropriation
(Budget Authority)

	Total Budget[a] ($M)	Drug Budget[b] ($M)	Drug Budget Share of Total (%)
SDFSC			
State grants	531.0	531.0	100.0
National programs	25.0	25.0	100.0
VVR grants	2,231.5	89.9	4.0
Special education			
Infants/families[c]	350.0	35.0	10.0
National acts[c]	279.0	0.2	0.0
NIDRR	76.8	0.5	0.7
Program administration	343.9	3.8	1.1
Other education department programs	30,883.3	0.0	0.0
Total	34,720.5	685.4	2.0

[a]This figure records the "Appropriation" as reported in the ED FY 1999 Budget Summary found at www.ed.gov/offices/OUS/Budget99/BudgetSum.

[b]These figures reported in ONDCP (1998b), pp. 36–37.

[c]ONDCP no longer includes Special Education programs in the federal drug-control budget.

Safe and Drug-Free Schools and Communities

ED counts all the state grants and national programs of the SDFSC program as drug prevention activities. This methodology has been used consistently since the publication of the first budget summary in 1990. A review of ONDCP documents suggests that changing the methodology was considered when Congress expanded the program's mandate to include antiviolence efforts. The 1995 budget summary noted that the violence prevention funds "will also have an impact on drug prevention." (ONDCP, 1995b, p. 44.) The following year, the budget summary stated the case more affirmatively, arguing that "all funds used under this program for violence prevention also have a direct impact on drug prevention." (ONDCP, 1996b, p. 92.)

That language has continued to be used to describe the SDFSC methodology.

VR and Grants for Infants and Families

For these two grant programs, the department attempts to identify the portion of program resources that serve clients suffering from the effects of illicit drug use. ED is careful to note that the methodology for VR is really an estimate:

> Although the budget identifies specific dollar amounts for treatment resources, these funds reflect only approximations of the cost of activities that assist individuals with a drug-related disabling condition. The Department estimates that approximately 4 percent of the Vocational Rehabilitation (VR) State grant funds will be used by State VR agencies to provide services to drug dependent clients for whom data are available—approximately 8.5 percent of individuals who achieved an employment outcome under this program had a primary or secondary disabling condition due to drug abuse. (ONDCP, 1998b, p. 37.)

This carefully qualified description of how VR funds are calculated has been used since 1994. ONDCP first reported the percentage used to calculate the drug-related portion of the VR program to be 1.5 percent in 1990 (ONDCP, 1990b, p. 146). That figure was revised upward in the 1991 summary to 3.4 percent (for FY 1990 and 1991). No justification was provided for the revision (ONDCP, 1991b, p. 187). Since then, the figure has slowly risen to the 4 percent currently used.

ED budget officials described the VR figure to be a "guesstimate" supported by empirical data (ONDCP, 1998b, p. 37). The department combines information from two data sets to produce the drug percentage. The first represents an estimate of the number of individuals served by VR programs for which drug abuse is the primary or secondary disabling condition. As noted above, this number was 8.5 percent for FY 1998. The second data set provides average cost estimates for the purchase of services for different disabling conditions. These data are derived from a sample of service providers. For the year in question, the cost of purchased services was slightly less than one-half that for other clients (47 percent). The product of the two numbers produces the 4 percent figure identified in the budget summary.

The department collects the client and cost data on a regular basis and uses the most recent data available to produce the drug-control estimates for budget submissions. Reporting lags, however, produce at least a two-year difference between the data used to produce the estimate and those for the budget year.

ED employed a similar approach to calculate the drug-related portion of the state grants for infants and families, estimating that 10 percent of the funds are spent on treatment activities for children who were prenatally exposed to drugs (ONDCP, 1998b, p. 37). As noted above, these programs are no longer scored as part of the antidrug budget. Department officials determined that the programs' contribution to drug treatment efforts was indirect and therefore suggested to ONDCP that it no longer be included in the totals. ONDCP agreed, dropping the Special Education programs beginning with the Fiscal Year 1999 budget summary.

NIDRR and Program Administration

For these activities, ED attempts to identify the specific projects or personnel that have an anti–illicit drug component. The cost of the grant or services provided is then tabulated individually as representing drug-control resources. For example, the NIDRR provides project grant funding for a variety of activities. According to ONDCP budget documents, projects with a clear, illicit drug focus are counted. It is more difficult to reconcile figures from the budget documents, in which drug-related funds were identified on essentially a case-by-case basis. Discussions and correspondence with department representatives, however, suggest that the methodology is appropriate.

The ONDCP budget summary reports that the NIDRR's drug-related activities fall under the Rehabilitation Research and Training Centers program. A review of the grant recipients reveals that of 46 awards, only one is focused on substance-abuse issues. This center, the Substance Abuse Resources and Disability Issues program at the University of Miami—Ohio School of Medicine, conducts research and provides training on issues related to "the intersection between substance abuse and disability conditions." (Substance Abuse Resources and Disability Issues Program, 2000.) The NIDRR lists the grant award at $499,000,[2] a number very close to the $500,000 reported in the ONDCP budget summary.

The department drug budget also includes the cost of administering these programs. In FY 1998, ED identified 34 FTEs responsible for overseeing drug and alcohol prevention programs. The compensation and benefits associated with these staff members are included in the drug budget (NIDRR, 2000). ONDCP documents report that the money associated with program administration represents the compensation and benefits of 34 FTEs. The budget summary reports drug-related program administration costs to be $3.788 million, or $111,000 per FTE. The latter figure appears to be low compared to program administration figures for the department as a whole. For FY 1999,[3] ED reported a total of $362 million for Program Administration, of which $202 million is salary and benefits and $160 million is for nonpay expenses. This number is associated with 2,664 FTEs (ED, 2000). Those figures would translate into $136,000 per FTE.

The department explains the difference by noting that its calculation is based on only a subset of the total program administrators, specifically those in the Offices of Elementary and Secondary Education and Special Education and Rehabilitation Services. Administrative costs for these programs tend to be slightly lower than those for some of the department's other areas (e.g., student aid processing, evaluations, and publications) (Scites, 1999). To the department's credit, it could have used a simpler, though less precise, approach by developing a per-FTE amount for all program administration. Instead, an additional step in the calculation attempts to account more accurately for the costs associated with drug-control program administration.

CONCLUSION

This investigation into ED's drug budget methodology raises some concerns regarding the degree to which it accurately reflects drug-control resources. In some instances, resources appear to be counted as antidrug programs when their effect on drug use and its consequences appears to be very indirect and/or limited.

---

[2]Figure found by searching the database of NIDRR grant recipients (see NIDRR, 2000).

[3]A comparable breakout of numbers was not available for FY 1998.

Counting SDFSC Grants as 100-Percent Prevention

The current methodology appears to overstate the amount of resources devoted to drug prevention, since funds used to improve school safety are included in the total.

When it originally established the Drug-Free Schools and Communities in 1986, Congress more narrowly defined the activities the program was to fund. The definition expanded when the program was reauthorized to include school safety. The 1994 statute suggests that SDFSC funds could be used to pay for metal detectors and security personnel. Although Congress clearly intended to support such activities when it revised the law, it is far less clear that these measures constitute drug prevention.

As noted above, the department maintains that the additional safety measures affect drug prevention. That effect, however, appears to be only potential and, at best, indirect. There is clearly a nexus between the distribution of drugs and violence. Also, not all violence is drug-related, and not all drug use results in violence. It is conceivable that increased security measures may have some deterrent effect on potential drug distributors by increasing the probability of a search. At the same time, a metal detector alone will not prevent drug use.

To determine whether it is appropriate to count all the SDFSC dollars as drug prevention, the department would need to determine the share of grant dollars being used for safety and security activities. Current law caps the amount of resources spent on school security equipment and personnel at 20 percent.[4] If all local education authorities were to use only half that amount (10 percent) on safety expenditures, the current methodology would overstate prevention resources by $50 million.

Department representatives note that precisely determining the share of the program's resources that is being used for safety activities could be costly in terms of time and resources for all organizations associated with the program. It is not clear, however, that a complete census of the program is necessary. Currently, a subset of SDFSC-funded programs is being evaluated. The department could

---

[4]See the Elementary and Secondary Education Act of 1994, Title IV, §4116.

"piggyback" an attempt to determine the distribution of resources between prevention and safety activities on such an evaluation effort. At a minimum, the department should have some defensible estimate of the portion of SDFSC funds being used for school safety and security.

Counting VR Grants as Drug Treatment

As department and ONDCP documents describe them, the activities the VR program funds appear to be drug related, but not drug-treatment related. Research does suggest that drug treatment programs that include such services as vocational training can improve outcomes. Such programs treat substance abusers first, however, then support that treatment with vocational training. As described in the budget documents, the VR program provides vocational training for clients, some of whom have a substance-abuse problem.

The goal of the VR program, then, is not necessarily to end or decrease the use of illicit drugs. Rather, it is to prepare clients for potential employment. The VR program may contribute to pursuing ONDCP Goal 3, but that contribution appears to be an indirect or supporting one.[5] Given that role, it is not appropriate to include the VR program in the federal drug-control budget as drug treatment. Such a move would be consistent with the earlier decision to drop Special Education Grants from the drug budget.

---

[5]It should be noted that the department does not attempt to present the VR as drug treatment, merely that the program serves a certain share of clients with drug problems.

Chapter Thirteen

CONCLUSIONS AND RECOMMENDATIONS

Is the President's National drug control budget an accurate representation of federal expenditures on antidrug activities? For the agencies reviewed, the answer is mixed. In three cases, the methodologies were appropriate and provided reasonable estimates of the resources being devoted to antidrug efforts. The other seven methodologies fell short. Some began with a systematic approach but did not apply it consistently or included funds that should not have been counted. Others lacked empirical foundation and/or were based on outdated information.

For these problematic cases, the ONDCP Director is not able to carry out his statutory responsibilities and cannot be certain whether the resources are available to achieve the objectives laid out in the strategy. He is not able to use the budgets to support particular priorities or hold agencies accountable for their performance. Most importantly, these methodologies do not provide Congress and the American people with an accurate picture of federal antidrug funding.

SUCCESSFUL METHODOLOGIES

The Coast Guard has developed a dynamic model for calculating antidrug expenditures based on a timekeeping system and on tracking the costs of these operations. This information is collected and reported quarterly. BOP compiles data each year on the percentage of its inmate population sentenced for drug offenses. That percentage is then multiplied by the total costs of salaries, expenses, modernization, and facility repair to determine the antidrug expenditures. In both these cases, the information is also used to project future antidrug expenditures. DOD, through its planning, programming, and budgeting system, determines which military assets will be dedicated to antidrug activities and then includes their costs in its counterdrug budget.

SYSTEMATIC APPROACH BUT FLAWED APPLICATION

Three of the agencies examined began with a logical framework for estimating drug expenditures, but the implementation fell short of producing reliable numbers.

The FBI's TURK system allows agents in one of its divisions, the OCE unit, to record the time spent on antidrug activities. The FBI calculates an overall percentage of time and assigns this percentage of its overall division costs to the antidrug budget. Problems arise in the other divisions, because the TURK system does not provide categories for recording the time their agents spend on antidrug activities. Consequently, the FBI has defined a complicated methodology based on judgments about the types of investigations that are "potentially" antidrug and then an extrapolation of data collected in the OCE unit. These other divisions constitute more than 60 percent of the FBI's antidrug budget.

Using empirical data, DVA identifies patients suffering from drug addiction and assigns the costs of their substance-abuse treatment to the antidrug budget. A significant problem emerges, however, when the department allocates the costs of other kinds of medical care for the same patients, for these conditions have little or nothing to do with their addiction.

ED uses client profiles and cost data to estimate the portion of its total budget that comprises antidrug services and grants. Some of the services programs provide, such as VR, may be drug related but do not provide drug treatment or prevention services. For SDFSC grants, the department considers all the funding to be antidrug, even though up to 20 percent of these expenditures can be used for violence prevention.

LACKING EMPIRICAL BASIS

Four agencies reviewed employed methodologies that either lacked an empirical basis for their calculations or used outdated information.

The INS developed its methodology in the early 1990s based on the educated guesses of program officials, budget analysts, and ONDCP staff about the relative share of the agency's workload attributable to antidrug activities. No effort has been made since to revise these estimates or introduce a timekeeping system.

The methodology SAMHSA uses is not based on any empirical data but, rather, is a collection of arbitrary assumptions and rules. For example, the agency assumes that all of its substance-abuse funding on Knowledge Development and Application activities is antidrug related, even though these activities cover illicit drugs, alcohol, and tobacco, as well as the abuse of prescription and over-the-counter drugs. Similarly, while claiming to focus narrowly on antidrug programs, SAMHSA includes funding for block grants for which the primary treatment is for alcohol and secondarily for drugs, as well as those that serve youth under 21 years of age.

The U.S. Customs Service bases its methodology on percentages that were initially developed by expert judgment with few empirical data. The agency annually makes some adjustments based on detailed programmatic knowledge, but the result is that it uses percentages that are inconsistent with what it presents publicly. No effort has been made to introduce a timekeeping system that can directly aid in budget development.

HCFA developed its methodology in 1989, based on patient diagnoses and costs. Since then, HCFA has revised the initial figures for inflation in medical costs and anticipated changes in the demand for services. The problem is that the patient data are taken from a 1983 survey, and no attempt has been made to introduce more-recent information.

SOME ANTIDRUG BUDGETS ARE INFLATED

What these methodological problems mean for the overall size of the antidrug budget is uncertain. It is not possible to say whether the budget figures for departments and agencies that fail to use current empirical data to determine antidrug expenditures are high or low. The reviews suggest that the Coast Guard and BOP reflect their antidrug resources quite accurately. DOD bases its estimates on the costs of assets allocated to the counterdrug operations. It does not, however, include the costs of most of the active-duty personnel involved, which has the effect of underestimating the overall amount of expenditures for the counterdrug effort.

In three cases, however, the methodologies used produce inflated antidrug budgets, the cumulative effect of which is to increase the overall FY 1998 antidrug budget of $16 billion by over $1 billion.

ED's antidrug budget identified $125 million worth of programs as being used to provide drug treatment services when they do not. These vocational programs and special education grants provide educational services, not drug treatment, for clients for whom drug abuse is a problem. Similarly, the SDFSC grant may overstate the resources designated for drug prevention. The entire $500 million program is included in the drug budget, even though up to 20 percent of the funds ($100 million) could be used for violence prevention activities, paying for such things as security personnel and metal detectors. The result is that the department's antidrug budget in FY 1998 may be inflated by as much as $225 million, or about 30 percent of its total stated drug budget.

The way SAMHSA calculates its drug budget produces a number that is considerably higher than its stated methodology would produce. The agency claims that its methodology is based on the percentages defined in the program's authorizing legislation, which includes a provision specifying a minimum expenditure (35 percent) for alcohol-only activities. In fact, the agency includes many such programs in its calculation of the antidrug budget. By applying the methodology it claims to use, the SAMHSA antidrug budget would be $250 million, or about 20 percent less than the one presented in the FY 1998 budget.

The largest discrepancy emerges in DVA. By including the other medical care costs for drug-abuse patients, its budget is inflated by up to $710 million, or 66 percent. These resources are reported as drug treatment when, in fact, the services rendered may have nothing to do with substance abuse.

For each of these agencies, the differences are significant. The effects of these overestimates are even more pronounced when one considers that these three agencies are all involved in programs to reduce the demand for drugs, either through prevention or treatment. In FY 1998, these programs totaled about $5.4 billion. Handicapped by a 20-percent margin of error in available resources, the ONDCP Director can neither effectively plan programs to reduce the demand for illicit drugs nor hold agencies accountable for their performance.

RECOMMENDATIONS

Given the difficulties these agencies have in compiling their drug budgets, the question arises as to whether ONDCP should continue to collect and present such a detailed budget. The answer rests on the role one wishes the ONDCP Director to play.

He could revert simply to presenting a federal drug-control budget table, without supporting detail, and acknowledge that it only approximates total expenditures. This would be easier and less time-consuming and would serve the political needs of an administration by showing a rise in the level of antidrug expenditures. ONDCP could still lobby for increased agency budgets in rough accord with the national strategy's objectives. Beyond this relatively shallow degree of participation in policy, ONDCP would have limited ability to administer antidrug programs.

Or the director could seek to manage the crosscutting antidrug programs. The legislative history of the office clearly indicates that Congress envisioned a management role for ONDCP. The powers of budget review and certification are central to it fulfilling that role.

The ONDCP Director will only be able to carry out his legislatively mandated responsibilities and use the budget to plan and hold agencies accountable by defining new methodologies to produce reliable budget figures. These recommendations specifically address the 10 agencies reviewed, but the general principles may be applied to all the agencies that report antidrug expenditures.

Methodologies Should Be Based on a Systematic Approach

While calculating a drug budget will necessarily be a function of estimates and assumptions, the process needs to be based on a systematic approach that is well documented, replicable, and reconcilable with other reported figures. The most important step in developing such an approach would be for ONDCP to define explicitly what constitutes an antidrug activity. Ambiguity exists today. The ONDCP antidrug budget purports to tabulate drug-control program costs as opposed to the health and social costs of illicit drug use. At the same time, one of ONDCP's goals is to "reduce the health and social costs of drug use" (Goal 3). After deciding, ONDCP should ensure that this definition is applied consistently within an agency and, to the extent possible, across all the antidrug agencies. At a minimum, for example, SAMHSA should use either the relatively broad definition of drug activities in its research grants (Knowledge and Development Application) or the narrow definition in its other programs, but not both.

Defining antidrug activities also raises the issue of whether to include the costs of services to individuals for alcohol abuse. ONDCP has long stated that, with the exception of alcohol use by those under the age of 21, its mandate is to focus on illicit drug use. So in DVA, the methodology makes adjustments to exclude individuals for whom alcohol is their only substance of abuse. While it may be possible mathematically to separate out drug abuse services from other substance-abuse services, such a distinction may not be relevant from a programmatic and management perspective.

An additional argument for a more-systematic approach can be found in what produced the three largely successful methodologies. The systems DOD (PPBS system) and BOP (Capacity Planning Committee) and the Coast Guard (resource utilization model) use for calculating their drug budgets were instituted for other purposes—planning and managing their multimission agencies. These systems also lend themselves to a systematic accounting of drug dollars. One would expect, then, that the reverse might be true. By approaching the counting of drug dollars more routinely, the agencies might realize other benefits in their overall efforts to manage their agencies and be motivated to institute overall systems.

Methodologies Should Be Empirically Based and Current

The drug-budget methodologies should be based on current empirical data, something more than expert judgment or best guesses. As important, the representation of the resources devoted to the antidrug effort should be accurate.

Toward this end, the Coast Guard's system of tracking how much time is spent on different missions provides a possible model for agencies involved in drug interdiction and law enforcement. The FBI's, which allows agents to record the time spent on different assignments, now needs to be expanded so that agents in all the units will be able to report the time they spend on antidrug investigations. Such a permanent and elaborate timekeeping system may be too costly for the INS and the Customs Service. Such a significant change, though, may not be necessary. These organizations could assess the time utilization of their personnel by periodically sampling a group of inspectors and investigators and/or the assets they use.[1] By conducting such a timekeeping audit at regular intervals, the agencies could identify how their resources are allocated to different program activities. This distribution could then be used to calculate the share of the budget devoted to antidrug efforts.

Grant-providing agencies could follow a similar strategy in attempting to gather empirical data on how the funds they distribute are used by the recipients. Requiring all recipients to report on every dollar they receive for the purposes of developing a drug-budget number would be overly burdensome for both the agencies and the recipients. Many of these grant programs, however, do have ongoing evaluations of a subset of their recipients. Including in these evaluations a component that attempts to assess how resources are being utilized relative to the categories in the federal drug budget does not appear to be onerous. In short, using empirical information collected from a sample of program participants would be more desirable than relying on a collection of percentages chosen in a relatively arbitrary fashion.[2]

Some agency representatives have suggested there is some merit to using consistent percentages over time, as has been the case with the INS and SAMHSA. They have argued that by keeping the percentages

---

[1]These agencies may already conduct similar audits, but no systematic efforts appear to be under way to gauge time utilization for these purposes.

[2]It is possible that a nonscientifically chosen sample of programs would produce a biased result and that expert judgment would yield a more accurate estimate of the share of antidrug efforts. Nevertheless, an approach that began with empirical data from a sample and then explained why that information may not accurately reflect the program as a whole would inspire more confidence.

constant, the process by which the drug budget is calculated becomes less time consuming and, at a minimum, enables some trend analysis. This rationale is not acceptable. Not revisiting these percentages means that the numbers will become more and more arbitrary and unrealistic as time passes. The policy and management decisions that are based on the drug budget necessitate a more precise set of numbers.

Similar Methodologies Should Be Derived from Common Principles

Each of the ten agencies used its own unique drug-budget methodology. No consistency existed overall or even in the cases of similar activities, such as law enforcement or treatment. In fact, budget officials in one organization were generally unaware of how other agencies calculated their drug budgets. ONDCP should work with the agencies to introduce more consistency in the way agencies calculate their drug budgets.

The introduction of common principles for developing drug budget methodologies suggests the need for categorizing the agencies, since no single approach would be appropriate for every organization. The most logical approach to emerge, as a result of this review, is to group the agencies by type of work performed, as a starting point for introducing more consistency in how agencies calculate their drug budgets.

- **Interdiction and law-enforcement agencies.** The Customs Service, Coast Guard, and INS all perform a similar interdiction function. DOD participates in a number of border interdiction and international efforts to disrupt traffickers. The FBI focuses more broadly, investigating and attempting to dismantle trafficking organizations. Drawing from the positive elements of DOD, FBI, and Coast Guard methodologies, the drug law-enforcement agencies, as a general rule, should first determine how their resources are deployed relative to their various missions. The shares should then be applied to the associated costs of the relevant assets and personnel.

- **Direct service providers.** In providing services, the DVA and BOP are faced with a variety of "clients" and must identify the individuals among them who are involved with illegal drugs. To calculate the drug budget, this type of agency must first differentiate among those who are and those who are not, and then account for the share of costs associated with providing services (e.g., inpatient treatment, incarceration) to those who are.

- **Grants which address multiple problems.** SAMHSA, ED, and HCFA provide grants to others, who then carry out the services. The challenge in accounting for drug dollars is to estimate how the recipients of the grants actually spend their funds. Some common guidelines can still be introduced. Agencies could, for example, choose to count services provided to all individuals suffering from addiction to both alcohol and illicit drugs (comorbidity) but exclude resources devoted to treating clients addicted only to alcohol. A more difficult issue is how to count prevention dollars. Should they be counted as 100-percent drug related, even though a significant component of their message is directed toward alcohol and nicotine? One possible approach would be to establish guidelines based on the substance and group being targeted. An anti-smoking or -drinking campaign directed at school children, for example, would be considered drug related because the substances are illegal for that population.

Public Presentation of Methodologies Should Be Consistent, Accurate, and Understandable

Each year, ONDCP publishes a budget summary to accompany the national strategy that it submits to Congress. The level of detail with which ONDCP presents these numbers and the accompanying narrative presented in the budget summary suggests a precise, systematic process. ONDCP also reports the methodologies as part of the budget summary.

Despite a considerable amount of detail, the budget summary does not contain sufficient information to enable an independent assessment of the methods used to produce the drug-budget figures. In many cases, the descriptions of these methodologies are relatively opaque and difficult to understand. In some cases, the methodology described in the budget summary simply does not reflect how the agency actually calculates the figures.

ONDCP should work with the agencies to ensure that the methodologies described in the budget summary are both accurate and understandable. This recommendation is qualified by the observation that a transparent, easy-to-understand methodology may not offer the most accurate estimate of antidrug expenditures. The INS' description in the budget summary is a straightforward set of percentages that can be reconciled relatively easily with figures publicly reported in other documents. This review revealed, however, that the percentages being used are based on "best guesses" made nine years earlier. A more complicated methodology, accompanied by a more-complicated description in the budget summary, would be preferable if it could produce a more accurate presentation of the drug budget. At a minimum, however, the methodology reported in the ONDCP budget summary should in fact be the one the agency uses.

BENEFITS OF IMPROVED METHODOLOGIES

Notwithstanding the costs of implementing these recommendations in terms of budget analysts and program officers developing workable procedures, significant benefits would result. By establishing some common principles to guide the agencies in developing their methodologies, ONDCP will be better positioned to compare the budgets of agencies performing similar tasks and to make trade-offs within budget limits. More consistency gives agencies an opportunity to learn from each other in their efforts to achieve more precision.

The most important benefit is that it will enable ONDCP to use the drug budget more effectively to implement strategies and hold agencies accountable for their performance. For FY 1998, the ONDCP Director presented the drug control budget as adequate to carry out the goals of its national strategy. But this review found inaccuracies in the representations of the antidrug expenditures and an overstatement of the resources available for demand-reduction programs. The efficacy of the planning process is thus called into question.

Given the nature of federal drug budget activities and the structure of the federal budget system, the drug control budget will necessarily be a collection of estimates, calculated using different methods, and involving the exercise of some discretion. But the reliability of its figures can be significantly improved. The basis from which these figures are derived can be made more transparent and understandable. This is essential for the ONDCP Director to be able to carry out his statutory responsibilities to direct and coordinate the nation's antidrug programs and for Congress and the American people to have confidence as to what resources are being spent on antidrug activities.

BIBLIOGRAPHY

21 USC §1703, National Drug Control Policy, Appointment and Duties of the Director and Deputy Directors, 1999.

21 USC §1705, National Drug Control Policy, Development, Submission, Imprementaiton, and Assessment of National Drug Control Strategy, 1999.

Elementary and Secondary Education Act of 1994, Title IV, §4121.

Elementary and Secondary Education Act of 1994, Title IV, §4116.

American Psychiatric Association, *DSM-IV Sourcebook*, Vol. I, Sec. 1, American Psychiatric Press, Inc., 1994.

Anshen, Melvin, "The Federal Budget as an Instrument for Management and Analysis," in David Novick, ed., *Program Budgeting: Program Analysis and the Federal Budget*, Cambridge, Mass.: Harvard University Press, 1965.

APA—*See* American Psychiatric Association.

BOP—*See* Federal Bureau of Prisons.

Bureau of the Budget, "Bulletin to the Heads of Executive Departments and Establishment: Planning-Programming-Budgeting (PPB), July 18, 1967," reprinted in James W. Davis, ed., *Politics, Programs, and Budgets: A Reader in Government Budgeting*, Englewood Cliffs, N.J.: Prentice-Hall, 1969, p. 179.

Carnevale, John, and Patrick Murphy, "Matching Rhetoric to Dollars: Twenty-Five Years of Federal Drug Strategies and Drug Budgets," *Journal of Drug Issues*, Vol. 29, No. 2, 1999.

Churchman, C. West, and A. H. Schainblatt, "PPB: How Can it be Implemented?" in Fremont J. Lyden and Ernest G. Miller, eds., *Planning Programming Budgeting: A Systems Approach to Management*, 2nd ed., Chicago: Markham Publishing, 1972, pp. 297–314.

Cohen, William S., *Report of the Quadrennial Defense Review*, May 1997. Available at http://www.defenselink.mil/pubs/qdr/ (last accessed August 31, 2000).

Commission to Assess the Organization of the Federal Government to Combat the Proliferation of Weapons of Mass Destruction, *Combating Proliferation of Weapons of Mass Destruction*, Washington, D.C.: U.S. Government Printing Office, July 14, 1999.

Customs—*See* U.S. Customs Service.

FBI—*See* U.S. Department of Justice, Federal Bureau of Investigation.

Federal Bureau of Prisons, *Summary Statement and Performance Plan, Fiscal Year 1999,*, 1999.

_____, "Federal Bureau of Prisons Quick Facts: Federal Prison Population Over Time/Drug Offenders," July 2000. See http:// www.bop.gov/fact0598.html#Drug (as of August 31, 2000).

Graham, B., "McCaffrey Blasts Pentagon for Spending on Drug War," *Washington Post*, November 7, 1997, p. A3.

Health Care Financing Administration, Cost of Drug Abuse to the Medicaid and Medicare Programs, internal memorandum, December 21, 1989.

Health Care Financing Administration, Medicaid Overview and Medicare Overview, FY 1998 enacted budget.. See http://www .hcfa.gov/ (as of November 8, 2000).

Immigration and Naturalization Service, budget submission to the U.S. Congress, FY 1999, 1998.

Lyden, Fremont J., and Ernest G. Miller, eds., *Planning Programming Budgeting: A Systems Approach to Management*, 2nd ed., Chicago: Markham Publishing, 1972.

Meissner, Doris, INS Commissioner, draft letter to ONDCP Director Barry McCaffrey, 1996.

Murphy, Patrick J., "Keeping Score: The Frailties of the Federal Drug Budget," Santa Monica, Calif.: RAND, IP-138, 1994.

National Institute on Disability and Rehabilitation Research program, Home page, May 30, 2000. Available at http://www.ed.gov/offices/OSERS/NIDRR/ (last accessed August 31, 2000).

Office of National Drug Control Policy, *National Drug Control Strategy*, Washington, D.C.: U.S. Government Printing Office, various years, a.

_____, *National Drug Control Strategy: Budget Summary*, Washington, D.C.: U.S. Government Printing Office, various years, b. Available at http://www.whitehousedrugpolicy.gov/budget98/agency-09c.html

_____, *Performance Measures of Effectiveness: A System for Assessing the Performance of the National Drug Control Strategy*, Washington D.C.: U.S. Government Printing Office, February 1998c.

ONDCP—*See* Office of National Drug Control Policy.

Public Law 105-20, Drug-Free Communities Act of 1997, June 27, 1997.

Public Law 105-277 §705 (d), Coordination with National Drug Control Program Agencies in Demand Reduction, Supply Reduction, and State and Local Affairs, Accounting of Funds Expended, October 21, 1998,

Public Law 102-321, Subpart II, Block Grants for Prevention and Treatment of Substance Abuse, §1921, Formula Grans to States, June 3, 1992.

Public Law 100-690, Anti–Drug Abuse Act of 1988, November 18, 1988.

Public Law 102-395, Department of Justice Appropriations Act of 1993, 1992.

Rubin, Irene, "Budgeting for Accountability: Municipal Budgeting for the 1990s," *Public Budgeting and Finance*, 16, 1996, pp. 112–132.

Reuter, Peter, "Setting Priorities: Budget and Program Choices for Drug Control," *University of Chicago Legal Forum*, 1994, pp. 145–173.

Schick, Allen, "The Road to PPB: The Stages of Budget Reform," in Lyden and Miller (1972), 1972a.

_____, "Systems Politics and Systems Budgeting," in Lyden and Miller (1972), 1972b.

Scites, Deborah, Department of Education, e-mail to Larry Cohen, August 4, 1999.

Substance Abuse and Mental Health Administration, *Congressional Presentation Document*, FY 1999.

_____, internal memorandum, December 1991.

_____, internal memorandum, January 1992.

Substance Abuse Resources and Disability Issues (SARDI) Program, home page, University of Miami—Ohio School of Medicine, August 31, 2000. Available at http://www.med.wright.edu/SOM/SARDI/ (last accessed August 31, 2000).

U.S. Bureau of Prisons, *Federal Bureau of Prisons Summary Statement and Performance Plan Fiscal Year 1999*, Washington, D.C.: U.S. Department of Justice, 1999.

U.S. Coast Guard, *Budget Estimates: Fiscal Year 1999, United States Coast Guard*, 1999a.

_____, "U.S. Coast Guard Description," paper received at meeting, February 26, 1999c.

_____, *Budget Estimates: Fiscal Year 1999, United States Coast Guard*, 1999b, p. 49 .

_____, *Fiscal Year 2000 Budget in Brief,* 2000, *p.* 28

_____, Web site, August 21, 2000. Available at http://www.uscg.mil (last accessed August 30, 2000).

U.S. Customs Service, *United States Customs Service FY 1999 President's Budget Justification Materials,* Washington, D.C.: U.S. Treasury, February 2, 1998.

_____ Web page, http://www.customs.ustreas.gov/about/mission .htm, 1999.

U.S. Department of Defense, *FY2000/01 Biennial Budget Estimates,* February 1999.

U.S. Department of Defense, About the Department of Defense and DefenseLINK, July 14, 2000. Available at http://www.defenselink. mil/admin/about.html (last accessed August 31, 2000).

U.S. Department of Education, web page, May 9, 2000. Available at http://www.ed.gov/offices/OUS/Budget99/ (last accessed August 31, 2000).

U.S. Department of Justice, Federal Bureau of Investigation, *FY99 Authorization and Budget Request for the Congress,* 1998.

U.S. Department of Veterans Affairs, *Department of Veterans Affairs FY 1999 Budget Submission,* Washington, D.C., 1998.

U.S. Senate, Judiciary Committee, "Report to Accompany the Nomination of Dr. William J. Bennett to be Director of National Drug Control Policy," Executive Report 101-2, March 9, 1989.

Wildavsky, Aaron, "The Political Economy of Efficiency: Cost-Benefit Analysis, Systems Analysis, and Program Budgeting," *Public Administration Review* 26, December 1966, pp. 292–310.